The Land and People

of

CANADA

FRANCES AILEEN ROSS

FOREWORD BY A. R. M. LOWER

𝔓𝔬𝔯𝔱𝔯𝔞𝔦𝔱𝔰 𝔬𝔣 𝔱𝔥𝔢 𝔑𝔞𝔱𝔦𝔬𝔫𝔰 𝔖𝔢𝔯𝔦𝔢𝔰

J. B. LIPPINCOTT COMPANY

PHILADELPHIA AND NEW YORK

Contents

◇◇

PORTRAITS OF THE NATIONS SERIES

Foreword
◇◇

THE CONTINENT of North America is seldom shown upon a map. Maps of the United States stop abruptly at the Great Lakes and the forty-ninth parallel, above which, as a rule, there looms empty space. Maps of Canada, perforce, take in adjoining regions of the United States, but simply as necessary marginal details. It is hard to find a map which shows the primary topographical divisions of the continent: the Appalachians are usually cut off sharply by the forty-fifth parallel, and the Canadian Shield terminated by the Rainy River. It is virtually impossible to get a map which recognizes even the weather as an international phenomenon: lines of temperature or rainfall are apparently halted at the border by the customs officials. In other words, until recently the United States has lived in a kind of ostentatious ignorance of Canada, and Canada has done its feeble but unsuccessful best to return the compliment.

Today the situation is changing. As long as Americans thought of Canada as a mere British colony, they associated it with the strifes of the Revolution, and dismissed it as a legendary realm of ice and snow which had once represented the old foe, but which time had proved harmless. Canadians, for their part, while unable to write off their vast and often seemingly dangerous neighbor, sought compensation in somewhat pharisaically attributing special righteousness to themselves, and in their secret hearts fought the American Revolution over again to a more successful outcome.

But now that Canada, as well as the United States, is growing up, these adolescent fits and piques are passing. Canada looks at the United States with the critical, but not unadmiring, eye of a younger brother. The United States is, perhaps, aware that there is another son in the house—or should one say, a second person sleeping in the bedroom?

As always, the printed word has had a large place in effecting these changes. It is therefore pleasant to welcome another book which contributes to international understanding, particularly when it does so as graciously and sympathetically as does the present volume. Miss Ross is helping us to mutual awareness. It is important to both North American peoples that to awareness there should be joined understanding, respect and good feeling. There are many ways of securing these desirable ends, but surely one of the most powerful is through good books—books which do not romanticize but attempt to describe their subject carefully, soberly, and truthfully. It is satisfying to turn to Miss Ross's work and find that Canada does not consist entirely in Mounted Policemen in scarlet tunics, "getting their man," but in ordinary North American people, very much like other Americans, though with their own traditions and loyalties. Miss Ross is to be commended for her fine effort to draw in the details on the northern half of the continental map.

A. R. M. Lower

United College,
Winnipeg, Manitoba.

Illustrations

◇◇

CHAPTER I

◇◇ *Canada Today* ◇◇

CANADIANS SEEM TO BE so like Americans that we frequently accept them unthinkingly, and we are sometimes surprised when they behave differently in like circumstances. They go to the same movies, listen to the same radio programs, dance to the same music, use similar money, play baseball—and Canada's hockey teams are too well known to United States fans to need any introduction. We exchange notables across the border with the greatest of ease. Norma Shearer, Mary Pickford, Walter Pidgeon, Raymond Massey, all were born in Canada, as were numerous American university presidents and professors, doctors of medicine, lawyers, and so forth. In fact, so many Canadians have filled notable positions in the United States as to lead to the well-known quip that Canada's chief export is brains. The number of United States citizens who have chosen to make Canada their home has not been correspondingly large. However, Canadians point to the Right Honorable C. D. Howe, the Minister of Reconstruction in the present Dominion cabinet, as an example of an American turned Canadian.

Americans form their opinions of Canada in terms of the part of that country with which they may be acquainted. Montreal and Quebec draw the tourist from eastern United States, and so to them Canada is French and "quaint." Americans of the Middle West vacation in Toronto, Winnipeg, or any of many cities in Ontario, and they, forming their opinions accordingly, see an English-speaking part of Canada relatively similar to their native states south of the border. Californians, Oregonians, and Washingtonians, travelling northward probably visit either Vancouver or Victoria. The former city, a thriving metropolis, might possi-

1

bly remind them of Seattle. If they visited Victoria, on the other hand, they would come away with the idea that Canada was "very English."

The boundary which separates Canada from the United States is little more than a line across the face of North America. The traveller stops at the border, it is true, for routine questioning, and, once across, he notices the Union Jack much in evidence. Billboards may advertise different products, and streets are likely to carry such names as "King," "Queen," or "Prince." But traffic laws are similar; buildings are of the same design. There is little to remind him that he is travelling in another nation, unless, by chance, he stops in some French village in Quebec and attempts to wrestle with the language difficulty.

Americans and Canadians alike are proud of their three-thousand miles of undefended boundary. Few of us realize that we disregard the line separating Alaska from Canada—another two thousand miles, also unfortified.

Although Canada is one-sixth larger than the United States, the latter has about twelve times as many people. The great majority of Canadians live within a hundred-mile band along the southern boundary of the country. For many years most of them were farmers, and they followed the fertile soil westward because the north was cold and forbidding, and a ledge of rock barred expansion in that direction. Actually, Canada is cut into two parts by a rocky cap, known as the Canadian Shield, which covers over two thirds of the country. It sweeps around Hudson Bay in a great semicircle, from Labrador to Great Bear Lake in the Northwest Territories. In the western part of Ontario it comes down to the Great Lakes. Until 1946 there was no through highway north of Lake Superior. It takes a day to cross this area by rail. Only a few dejected-looking settlements break the otherwise uninterrupted stretch of forests and streams and still more forests, hour after hour in monotonous succession.

The countryside of Canada looks the same as that of the United

States. With the exception of the Great Lakes, the major geographical barriers run north and south. The Appalachians continue to the water's edge of the Gulf of St. Lawrence, to separate the Maritime Provinces from the rest of the country. The Rockies extend through Canada to the Arctic Circle, to isolate British Columbia from the East. The Maritime Provinces are a continuation of northern New England; parts of Ontario are similar to western New York and Ohio; the Middle West of the United States becomes the prairies in Canada; and British Columbia is a northern extension of Oregon and Washington.

Canada is divided into nine provinces, and two territories. Just as the states which make up the United States tend to be grouped together because of common interests—New England, Middle Atlantic, Southern, Middle Western States, and so forth—so Canada falls into well-defined regions, five in number. Beginning with the eastern part of the country, Nova Scotia, New Brunswick, and Prince Edward Island are known as the Maritime Provinces. Commercially they are closely affiliated with the New England States, especially Maine and Massachusetts. Here the population is more equally distributed than is the case with the other six provinces. This region is older than the rest of the country, except for Quebec. Quebec and Ontario, taken together, form Central Canada. Although classed together, these two provinces are dissimilar in most respects. They are divided by race, religion, and customs. Quebec is French-speaking and Roman Catholic; while Ontario, English-speaking and Protestant, is probably the most bitterly anti-French of all the provinces. We group them together on the basis of commerce and geography. Both are highly industrialized and located in the center of Canada. Manitoba, Saskatchewan, and Alberta taken together form the Prairie Provinces, the "bread-basket" of Canada. The soil is very fertile, and experimentation has produced a fine strain of wheat which commands top prices in the markets of the world. British Columbia stands alone as the fourth zone. Her geographical connection with the rest of Canada is an artificial one, a matter of four railway lines through the mountains. Many European nations would give much to possess so formidable a boundary as the Rocky Mountains.

North of the provinces the land is sparsely settled. For purposes of government it is divided into two territories. The Yukon, adjoining Alaska, was the scene of the famous gold rush in the nineties, which precipitated the Alaska boundary dispute. Out of a population of over twenty-seven thousand in 1901, less than five thousand people remain. Most of the early settlers have returned to sunnier climes; many of the others have taken up lumbering or agriculture. The Northwest Territories are empty and largely unexplored. About nine thousand Indians and Eskimos are scattered along the rivers and the coast. Until recently, agents of the government or the Hudson's Bay Company and a few missionaries made up most of the white population. The opening of mines around Great Bear and Great Slave lakes has led, in recent years, to an influx of miners and prospectors.

The people of Canada are more sharply divided than those in the United States. Although the American "melting pot" has not completely melted, its contents have softened and mingled somewhat. In Canada the division between French and English has produced two languages, two sets of customs and traditions, and two religions. The French regard themselves as the oldest white inhabitants of Canada. Why should they adopt British ways? The Roman Catholics of British origin fulfill their religious obligations strictly enough but they refuse to be dominated by the French clergy of Quebec.

A Canadian travels less than the average American. As a result, each region is more proudly conscious of its own individuality. Before the war shuffled so many servicemen hither and yon, many people had never visited other sections of the country. Folks in Winnipeg, for instance, could probably tell you more about Minnesota or Wisconsin than about eastern Ontario or Quebec. It costs a lot of money to travel across Canada. (From coast to

coast by rail takes a full day longer than in the United States.)
People from Toronto can reach New York in about a third of the
time it takes to go to Halifax. Under normal conditions, a Nova
Scotian could see England more cheaply than the Canadian
Rockies and British Columbia. Even Montreal, which we think
of as being near the center of the country, is closer by plane to
Scotland than to Vancouver. The distances are simply tremendous, and one of the great problems for Canadians has been to get
to know each other.

Wherein are Canadians different from Americans? Well, they
are very proud of their relationship to Britain and of their independent status in the British Commonwealth of Nations. They
often dislike Englishmen as individuals and resent the patron-
izing air which they too frequently adopt when talking of the
"colonies." But to the British tradition of democracy and freedom
they are fiercely loyal. They tend to bridge the gap between Britain and the United States. Although they are more like Americans than they are like the British, they have some characteristics
not common in the average United States citizen. Canadians are
inclined to be more conservative and deliberate than Americans.
Sometimes they are over cautious. When pitchblende was discovered in the Northwest Territories, for instance, Toronto mining
circles were interested, but not to the extent of putting up enough
money to finance the company. It was the United States investor
who was willing to gamble on a mine near the Arctic Circle!

CHAPTER II

❖ *The People* ❖

Most Americans, and some Canadians even, if asked the racial origins of the people of Canada, would reply, "Why, English and French!" They would be right, but only up to a point, for there are people from many European countries in Canada—thirty national groups in all. Their presence is not noticed in the eastern part of the country because they are lost among the English and French who outnumber them many times. Once in the Prairie Provinces, however, Slavic and German features are a common sight. The local newspapers carry stories of the folk dances and music at the New Canadian Festival in Regina. In the outlying countryside, small settlements clustered around a Lutheran church or a church of Eastern design with its onion-shaped dome, are a strong reminder that about one-fifth of the people known today as Canadians came from Germany, Czechoslovakia, Poland, the Ukraine, and the Scandinavian countries, to mention only a few.

Because of the severity of the Canadian winter, government officials did not encourage the immigration of Europeans from the Mediterranean area. They felt it wiser to populate Canada with those already accustomed to the cold. Even so, sizeable groups of Italians and some Greeks live in the cities and towns of eastern Canada.

To distinguish them from the earlier settlers, the newcomers are frequently called "New Canadians." Those of French origin are known as French Canadians, while all whose roots go back to the British Isles are loosely spoken of as English Canadians—though originally they may have been Scottish, Irish, or Welsh.

Comparatively few people in Canada today were born in the British Isles—only about eight per cent. As the word "American" is used in the United States to describe citizens of that country, so a Canadian is a thoroughly North American product. He too has been forced to adapt himself to a life very different from that of his ancestors, and his behavior is more frequently "American" than British or European.

The French have lived in and loved the Canadian countryside longer than any other people. Since the middle of the eighteenth century they have had little contact with France. Their pleasures, anxieties, and problems have revolved about their home, their church, and their parish. They treasure no strong devotion for France. It has been by their own efforts, and not because of her help, that they have preserved their way of life. France, to the French Canadians, is part of the romance of the distant past, and not the object of their present loyalty. They are "Canadiens," and their allegiance is strongly Canadian.

The English, Scottish, Irish Canadians are in a somewhat different position. They also are truly Canadian in outlook and action, devoted to their country and eager to develop it. However, whatever may have been their reason for coming to Canada, they have maintained contact with Britain. Frequently distant members of a family still live there; or for reasons of business and finance there is a constant coming and going between the two. The proportion of English Canadians is decreasing. They made up slightly less than half the total population at the last census, and their numbers will probably continue to decline unless the birth rate rises, or sizeable imigration from the British Isles is resumed.

Most of the "New Canadians" have come from lands where oppression and suffering had been their lot. They welcomed the opportunity of free homesteads in the Canadian wilderness of the West. While some of them may not yet have learned how to use to the best advantage their newly found freedom, the great majority are grateful to an indulgent government for the liberty that is now theirs—to live their own lives, to preserve their individual customs, to worship their God as they may choose. They have labored diligently, endured great hardships, and are becoming good citizens. Many have learned to speak English, and to the second generation growing up, Canadian ways are natural.

Popular fancy pictures the French Canadian as a farmer, with a very large family, living in a little white house, one of many in a long row, set side by side along the river bank; his land, and that of his neighbors, stretching up the incline behind in narrow ribbonlike strips. The past twenty years have seen great changes in the countryside of Quebec. Manufacturing has moved in, as have large pulp and paper companies, clothing and metal industries. The farms are still occupied, the families still large, the land still worked in the ribbonlike strips, but the province has become urban.

In the early colonial days the French government and the Church discouraged the people from a life of trapping in the wilderness. They sought to build up the population in New France. In order to populate the countryside they made huge grants of land to certain individuals, called seignieurs, with the understanding that the land be parcelled out to tenant farmers, or habitants. Each habitant family paid the seignieur annually a certain fixed amount, in goods and days of labor. Long after England assumed control of the country, the seigniorial system remained in force. The example of the British farmer, working his own land independently, made the French demand the same system.

There are now few tenant farmers among the French. Some of them may be poor, but they are thirfty and what they have they own. The French farmer loves the soil and takes great pride in his farm. Each year his house receives a fresh coat of whitewash; and it is a matter of principle with him to pass on the farm in as good or better condition than he received it.

The French have large families. In early days, with land to be cleared and a score of chores to be done, many hands were necessary. They are still useful. The French farmer rarely hires help. The entire family, including quite small children, turn to with a will for the ploughing, seeding, harvesting, and other endless tasks of farm life. However, the matter of providing for these numerous children has become a major problem. They are trained for farm life and spend their youth working to build up a farm which they must leave as soon as they grow up. (Only one of them can remain.) Formerly, vacant land was available, and with thrift and hard work it was possible to create another farm. The situation has altered. The good farming land is completely occupied. Consequently, the father is forced to choose from among his family one son to inherit the place and to carry on the family name and tradition. If he has been reasonably successful, he may have enough money to send a second son to study for the priesthood. One or more daughters may enter a convent. The others drift off to the lumber camps or the pulp mills, to the textile factories or the mining regions of the North.

Rural Quebec contains few English-speaking people. Whole parishes are completely French and Roman Catholic. The same families live on, generation after generation, in the same parish and on the same farm. A parish consists of a number of families all belonging to one church. They not only belong to the church, but each family owns a pew and makes a definite, specified contribution—known as a tithe—in goods or money, to the value of one twenty-sixth of the annual grain income. The priest, or curé, of the parish directs the spiritual life, and often the worldly affairs of his flock. Frequently he is the son of a farmer from a neighboring parish. His youth was like theirs, he is one of them; he knows and shares their problems.

The Quebec farm usually provides the family with most of its food, its fuel, and, in some cases, its clothing. As cities have grown in population, the adjacent farms have turned to market gardening, and the money thus obtained has been used to provide for many of the family's needs. The art of woollen and linen weaving, formerly an important feature of country life, has been largely lost—to be slightly revived in recent years for the tourist trade!

Until the twentieth century, farm life was typical of the great majority of French families. The Industrial Revolution reached Quebec late. For many years its abundant water power went unharnessed. Now the forests of Quebec are being used to turn out paper for the American newsstands; its metals are being processed for the world markets; its textile mills provide clothing for several million Canadians.

Unlike the older industries which were small and owned and operated by the French themselves, these new industries are large multi-million-dollar affairs owned and managed by English, American, or English Canadian capital. The lack of farm land and the increasing population have driven many members of the large families into factory work. They live crowded in cheap tenements, for the industrial areas of Quebec differ from any similar American city only in that the people are poorer, more crowded, and less healthy. Wages in Quebec are lower, hours are longer, and safety conditions less well developed than in any comparable industrial center elsewhere in Canada. As a result, the health conditions of the people are wretched. Gone is the possibility of owning property, so dear to the pride of the French farmer. Quebec offers possibly the last happy hunting ground for manufacturers who can gloat over their profit-and-loss statements with little fear of labor leaders. However, the workers are beginning to awaken. Many of them are now aware that they receive fewer advantages than workers elsewhere. Some of them have joined labor unions affiliated with the AFL or the CIO. However, organized labor is still in its infancy in Quebec and must battle determined opposition from both provincial government and Church leaders. The former is impressed by the present "prosperity" of the province and fears that organized labor will discourage future industrial expansion, with a consequent shrinking of tax receipts. To the clergy, labor unions are Communist inspired. They threaten to undermine the teachings of the Church and the spiritual life of the people. As such they have no place within the framework of Roman Catholic life, and they must be prevented whatever the consequence.

Four people out of every five are French, and because of their numerical superiority they control the government. Elsewhere in Canada, British influence dominates, and English Canadians hold the most important posts in finance and industry.

The English Canadians moved to Canada in the wake of the army which conquered New France. The habitants, as conquered people, remained on their farms while many of the French ruling class returned to France. The British seized the opportunity to win control of the fur trade. From that profitable occupation they moved into others equally rewarding. They organized banking; they secured financial backing to build railroads and canals; they financed the bringing in of new settlers to people the West; they built factories and hydroelectric plants; they provided the impetus to realize the wealth contained in the rocks of the Canadian Shield.

The French, on the other hand, for many years were content with their land and absorbed by the struggle to preserve their mode of life, their language, customs, and religion against the growing tide of British influence. When they awakened to what was happening, the English were already established in all the major financial and industrial fields.

Life in an English Canadian family is similar to that of a corresponding family in the United States. Almost half of the people live on farms. The English Canadian farmer is like his "cousin" in the United States. He uses electricity, tractors, and harvesters when he can afford them. Sometimes he coöperates with his neighbors to buy more expensive equipment or to market his crops. His financial status varies, depending upon whether his soil happens to be fertile or rather poor. He complains about the low prices he receives for his produce in comparison with what he has to pay for goods in the stores.

In the towns and cities English Canadians go in for business or the professions. They may work in banks or offices; they may own stores and factories; they may be carpenters, plumbers, factory workers, any of scores of occupations. Many become professional men and women—doctors, clergymen, educators, engineers, lawyers. When they can afford it, and many of them seem to be able to, they own an automobile, perhaps a cottage on a lake or at the seashore. They like to spend a holiday in New York, Detroit, or Seattle when they can. The men join the Rotary Club, or the Masonic Order, or the IOOF. The women belong to clubs and institutes, for like women in the United States they enjoy a great measure of freedom. Fewer Canadian women hold high business and professional posts, but the entering wedge has been made and their numbers are constantly growing.

Schools in Canada are similar to those in the United States. All of the provinces provide public education in the elementary and secondary grades. In addition, there are private schools for such as have the money and inclination to attend. Canada has many universities—all of the larger ones, coeducational. Two have achieved wide recognition, McGill University in Montreal and the University of Toronto. Quebec has two French-language Universities, Laval in Quebec and the University of Montreal. The former has become outstanding in North America for the study of French literature.

Quebec province has a dual system of schools—Roman Catholic and Protestant. The Roman Catholic Church directs the education of the large majority of the population, while the English Canadian minority are provided with separate schools under the supervision of a Protestant school commission. The money allotted for education is divided between the two groups on the basis of population. The Protestant schools follow the familiar pattern which we know so well—kindergarten, elementary and high school.

The overwhelming majority of Roman Catholic children in Quebec are French Canadian. In many villages the entire population is French. All classes are conducted in that language. When English is taught, which it often is not, it is as a foreign language.

French Canadian ideas on education differ from those held by English Canadians or Americans. While higher education carries great prestige, it is considered to be a privilege reserved for the few, rather than a right to be enjoyed by many. Its necessity is recognized in order to prepare for the Church, for medicine, or for law—but not for the average person. Generally speaking, it is beyond the wildest imagination of the habitant farmer to be able to provide money to educate a large family, and he does not see the necessity of elaborate expenditures for public schools. If he can afford to educate one of his children, he gladly pays the bill—few students "work their way" through college in Quebec.

In the rural districts, schools are usually of the one-room variety. Only in 1943 did the Quebec legislature pass a law requiring students to stay in school until they are fourteen. Among poor families few remain after that age. Many teachers belong to religious orders and, consequently, receive no wages. The bountiful supply of clerical instructors makes the financial lot of the ordinary teacher exceptionally bad. Recently the minimum wage in the French Catholic schools has been raised from $400 to $600 a year, and many economical school boards will pay no more!

If the family is one with money and social position, the children are educated entirely in private schools. One or more of the boys go on to a Roman Catholic university. The others are sent to learn business practices in a specialized school. One son will undoubtedly follow his father's profession. (The French have been especially successful as lawyers.) The girls go to one of the many convents to be taught needlework, music, art, and possibly some shorthand and typewriting. The latter provides them with a useful occupation—in the few years before they marry—not in the business world, but working for their father or one of his friends.

Among the older settlers there are those who feel that the Canadian government made a mistake when it encouraged Central European groups to settle in the country. They point to the Doukhobors, Poles, or Ukrainians and say, "Those people are not Canadians! They aren't trying to be Canadians! They live in groups of their own nationality, speak their native tongue. Why, its disgraceful!"

True, they do tend to keep by themselves, and at home they speak Polish or Ukrainian as the case may be. The older women stay on the farm, see few people outside their family, and frequently never learn English. The older men learn enough to be able to get what they need in a store. However, many of them take education very seriously, not for themselves, for they feel too old, but for their children. The latter are going through the public schools and are learning the English language and customs. Already they have produced some professional men. Given another generation, they will be fairly thoroughly adapted to Canadian life. Also, interestingly enough, their adaptation will be to the language and customs of the English, rather than the French Canadians, for the influence of the former is much the stronger in the West.

The eastern European peoples love the soil. They make excellent pioneers. The greater the hardship, the more devoted they become to their farms. The Poles and Ukrainians, for instance, chose apparently unproductive bushland considered suitable only for berrying. They cleared it slowly, a few acres a year, using the fallen trees for fuel. Due to their industry and thrift, they are the proud owners of comfortable farms.

The Doukhobors, or "Spirit Wrestlers," are undoubtedly the most interesting group in western Canada. Originally, as pacifists, they refused to take part in war and ran afoul of military conscription in Russia in the 1880's. They were not members of the Orthodox Russian Church, but believed in a religious faith of their own devising. They held all their possessions in common, and were vegetarians. Actually, without police, lawyers, doctors, or ministers, they had achieved a social life free from crime and legal disputes. In addition, they were devoutly religious and exceptionally healthy. The Society of Friends became interested in their case and the Canadian government offered them free homesteads together with immunity from military service. The great majority, after they arrived in Canada, forsook communal living, took the oath of allegiance, and acquired homesteads. They sent their children to school and otherwise conformed to the ways of the country. Unfortunately, a small number of them have not adapted themselves to Canadian life. These have given the entire group a bad name and have made it the object of widespread amusement. Colorful, tempermental, intensely religious, they are seized by visions at the most unexpected times. (Or some action on the part of the Canadian government arouses their displeasure.) They become violently excited and tramp around the countryside or down a city street—it makes little difference to them— totally naked. The police dutifully round them up and lodge them in the jail. Quiet is restored.

The European people have many charming customs and valuable traditions to contribute to Canadian culture. They are now being encouraged to take pride in their folkways and to continue them. Their peasant embroidery is displayed at the annual festivals. They are fond of singing. Whenever a few gather together it becomes an occasion for music. While their folk dances are charming, their choral singing is amazing. They use no printed score and sing in perfect unison. Some years ago, the western provinces began the policy of having competitive musical festivals. Each group, in its native costume, was encouraged to participate. Already these festivals have helped to break down the barriers between races. Some enjoy singing, some enjoy being the audience, and they all come away with increased respect not only for their own heritage but for that of the others as well.

CHAPTER III

◇◇ *The Maritime Provinces* ◇◇

CANADA'S THREE SMALLEST PROVINCES, Nova Scotia, New Brunswick, and Prince Edward Island, border on the Atlantic Ocean. Geographically they represent a continuation northward of the Appalachian Mountains. However, although hilly over considerable areas, the land cannot be described as mountainous. Nova Scotia is cut into two parts by the Strait of Canso; it is both a peninsula and an island. Prince Edward Island is Canada's smallest province—about one hundred and forty miles long and from four to thirty-four miles wide. Though larger than Rhode Island, by Canadian standards it is a midget province. Both Nova Scotia and Prince Edward Island retain a strong Scottish flavor. New Brunswick, settled by Loyalists who fled from the wrath of the American patriots during the Revolutionary War, shows a rapidly growing French population.

It is a beautiful countryside—a countryside of contrasts. Here, yachting, hunting, fishing, swimming, camping and motoring provide an ideal playground for vacationers. Even the climate, in summer, seems to coöperate, with its cool, bracing, salt air, its gentle winds, and its clear, sunny skies. With rod and reel to Guysborough County or northward to the Restigouche River for salmon; deep into the forests of New Brunswick for moose and deer; to Chaleur Bay, the Bras d'Or Lakes, or the South Shore of Nova Scotia for yachting! The Maritime Provinces provide a spot to suit many moods—companionship or solitude, civilization or wilderness, pastoral quiet or rugged grandeur.

On the South Shore of Nova Scotia or in Cape Breton, high cliffs echo the thunder of surf upon a rocky shore. Along the

Cabot Trail, visited each year by the more venturesome, are rugged hills with correspondingly deep ravines, blanketed in evergreens; high rocky cliffs dropping sheer to the sea, and a winding road that leads around breath-taking curves through out-of-the-way Cheticamp and Cap Rouge where the traditions of the early French settlers live on in their descendants—and thence to Baddeck. There, unless one has nerves of iron, is welcome rest, with some boating and perhaps a visit to Beinn Bhreagh, the residence and final resting place of Alexander Graham Bell.

Before leaving Cape Breton, if one is interested in the past, a visit to Louisburg is in order. That mighty fortress, now a crumbling ruin, recalls the days when France, at the pinnacle of her power, sought to guard the approach to her empire on the St. Lawrence from English raiders.

Along the Northumberland Strait or the Bay of Fundy the countryside is sheltered by a range of hills which extends lengthwise through Nova Scotia. Rolling, fertile, river valleys are dotted with small towns and well-kept farms. The St. John River winds through its four-hundred-mile course from the Maine-New Brunswick boundary to the Bay of Fundy. This river valley, the longest in the Maritimes, is famed for its distinctive charm and beauty. Near its mouth the river rushes through a narrow, rocky gorge where twice a day the "reversing falls" turn and fall backward as the mighty Fundy tides push their waters upstream. The tides of the Bay of Fundy, as they push inland, form walls of water called "bores." The most famous bore occurs near Moncton on the Petitcodiac River where the tide rises nearly sixty feet.

Spring comes earlier to the Annapolis Valley, and with it come the apple blossoms. Apple Blossom Sunday in the Land of Evangeline opens the tourist season, and highways are thronged with people who drive for miles along roads seemingly cut through a fragrant, pink sea of blossoms. There, in their midst, at Grand Pré, the visitor pauses to pay tribute to the little French maid whom Longfellow immortalized.

A second stop is made at Annapolis Royal to see Fort Anne, known in the days of the French as Port Royal—the site of one of the earliest settlements in Canada. The main building has been replaced, but the earthwork remains as it was in those far-off days when France and England battled each other for possession of the continent.

Then, on to Grenville, where the De Monts and Champlain built a settlement, the Habitation, in 1605. The original buildings were demolished in 1613, but reproductions have been recently rebuilt and one can stroll through the courtyard and into halls that conform faithfully to the specifications of the early records.

The French were the first to colonize Nova Scotia and New Brunswick. Settling in the sheltered harbors along the Bay of Fundy, they built dikes to reclaim the marsh lands and established prosperous farms. Although France lost the mainland of Nova Scotia to England in 1713, the latter made no attempt to settle the country and the French farmers lived on undisturbed for many years. Finally, at the insistence of New Englanders who lived in constant terror of attacks from Louisburg, Sir Edward Cornwallis came out in 1749 with some twenty-five hundred settlers to found a fortress at Halifax. The newcomers found life more difficult than they had anticipated and many slipped away to New England. The ones who remained, old soldiers and sailors from the prisons and slums of England, were largely a shiftless, drunken, troublesome lot. Although some New Englanders soon came north, their value was not at first apparent, and wholesale recruitment was carried on, especially in Germany. (George II, the King of England, was a Hanoverian.) Several hundred Germans were brought over from the Palatinate. After a brief sojourn in Halifax, many moved to Lunenburg on the South Shore, where their thrift and industry soon produced a substantial community.

The English and French in Nova Scotia did not get along well together, nor for that matter did the two races get along anywhere together. After the English occupation, the French farmers continued to go their own way as though no change had occurred. They were reluctant to take an oath of allegiance to the English king. They minded their own business, wishing only to be left to themselves, but they disregarded the orders of officials in Halifax. The story of their expulsion, as it is called, has been graphically told in Longfellow's *Evangeline*. Crowded on ships, they were transported many miles and scattered throughout the American colonies. Many people have blamed the British government for the suffering these folk were forced to endure. Few realize that New England was the moving force behind this mass expulsion and that the Halifax officials disregarded specific orders from England to treat the French with consideration and to avoid any unpleasantness. Although many of the Acadians returned years later, their choice lands had been appropriated by others and they were forced to be content with less desirable holdings. There now remains little visible trace of French civilization in the Annapolis Valley, save a small memorial park containing a church and statue of Evangeline.

Although deprived of their earliest homes in Acadia, French communities may be found near Yarmouth and in Cape Breton. Over a third of the people in New Brunswick are French and their numbers are increasing yearly. Especially is this true in the north where the overflow from Quebec has been gradually penetrating deeper and deeper into the province.

To the Maritimes came many Scots, driven from their beloved Highlands by the repressive measures taken in retaliation for their loyalty to Bonnie Prince Charlie, claimant to the throne of England. The northern coast of Nova Scotia along the Northumberland Strait was still unoccupied, and a Scots settlement grew up in and around Pictou. Many more journeyed to Cape Breton Island because it reminded them of their homeland, with its wild hills, its deep ravines, its lakes and its crags. There, in remote communities, even today, their descendants can be heard still speaking the Gaelic, native language of the Scot. Although the kilt has been put aside in favor of more practical attire, it is still preserved and cherished, to be worn for the annual Highland Games or the St. Andrew's Day celebration. And many a German soldier of the first World War recalls with a shudder his encounter with these wild lads from the mountains who rushed into battle at the call of the pibroch.

The American Revolution sent many Loyalists—known to the Patriots as Tories—northward, with such small possessions as they could assemble. Members of many noted colonial families—the Winthrops, Saltonstalls, Putnams, and Winslows, found sanctuary in the then forbidding wilderness of the North. Some stayed in Nova Scotia, but more settled along the southern shore of what is now New Brunswick. Although they were all refugees from the wrath of the American patriots and the Continental Congress, Benedict Arnold's entry into their midst caused much displeasure. So cool was his reception by the Tories whose cause he had befriended that, after a short unhappy stay in Saint John, he moved on to London, to live out his life in disillusionment.

The Maritime Provinces are separated from the rest of Canada by the mountainous area of northern New Brunswick, and the Gaspé Coast. Today the railway and the airplane have spanned this obstruction but for many years the three provinces by the sea were forced to be independent and self-reliant. Their isolation from the rest of Canada was less difficult than might be expected. In many ways they enjoyed greater protection than did their sister provinces. With the founding of Halifax in 1749 by Sir Edward Cornwallis, uncle of the general of Yorktown fame, that harbor became the base for the North Atlantic Fleet, and the inhabitants felt secure in the protection of the British Navy.

Unable to maintain contact and trade with Canada, they found markets for their goods in Britain and the New England colonies. They maintained close economic ties with the latter even after the American Revolution. Although the railroad eventually joined the Maritimes with Quebec, excessive freight rates made extensive trade impractical. New England is still a great market for Maritime exports, and as Ontario wags frequently remark, "Boston is the capital of the Maritimes!"

Prince Edward Island is noted for its fur farms. Although larger farms now exist in the other provinces of Canada, it was here that the first foxes were raised in captivity for the commercial market. A fox farm consists of an enclosure surrounded by a high fence. Inside are pens made of wire netting laid out in blocks and streets. The wire netting is buried several feet under the ground and rises to a height of about eight feet to prevent the foxes from digging or climbing their way to freedom. In each pen is a kennel made from boards.

Foxes are born in the spring. Frequently young foxes must be taken from their mother, for in case of fright she is likely to kill them. Throughout the summer they are covered with a thin, shaggy coat of fur. With the coming of the cold weather, they lose their original coat and grow the beautiful heavy coat so highly prized by the furriers. When the fur is at its best, the foxes are put to sleep painlessly, by gas, and their pelts find their way to the large international fur market in Montreal. There was a time when a pair of fine foxes brought as much as $25,000. Such prices are no longer paid, however, because competition has made the fox industry expand to sizeable proportions. Fox farming has proved so successful that fur farmers now raise other animals such as mink, and to a lesser extent, marten, and chinchilla in similar fashion. The Dominion government conducts an experimental station at Summerside, P.E.I., in order to study the habits and needs of these animals, especially foxes.

The sea, in early days their only channel of transportation and a major source of food, still draws many sailors for a livelihood. In the days of the wooden ships, Britain encouraged lumbering because masts, spars, and timber were essential to her continuing sea power. Nova Scotia and New Brunswick prospered on the basis of these industries. The former was one of the leading ship-building centers of the world until steam replaced sail in the latter part of the nineteenth century. Donald MacKay, later to become immortal in seafaring annals for his construction of the *Flying Cloud* was but one of many Nova Scotians to "graduate" from instruction in its shipyards.

In New Brunswick energetic settlers were known to have built ships, loaded them with lumber, sailed them to England where they sold the entire outfit, and returned to repeat the process. With the discovery of gold in Australia there was suddenly a great demand for ships, for the English builders could not turn out vessels fast enough to accommodate the number of people wishing to go to the South Pacific. The great timber ships from New Brunswick were bought up, refitted, painted, and sent southward laden with eager gold seekers.

Although Saint John and Halifax have excellent, ice-free harbors, most of the peacetime trade with Europe is handled through Montreal and Quebec in order to avoid the costly rates of rail transportation to and from the Maritimes. In winter when the St. Lawrence is closed to shipping the eastern ports come to life. In wartime, Halifax teems with activity. Her harbor becomes a haven for the ships of all the allied nations, and sailors in their distinctive uniforms throng the streets.

Fishing, then as now, has always provided a considerable share of the income of Nova Scotia. Her coastline is very irregular, and practically every little inlet contains a fishing village. Tuna, salmon, and lobster find a ready sale throughout the markets of the world. However, the great fishermen of Nova Scotia are deep-sea fishermen. Out from Lunenburg sails a mighty fleet, the last of the Bluenose fishermen, on its way to the Grand Banks of New-foundland for cod. They own their own schooners. They have built them with their own hands from native lumber. Out in the Atlantic they battle fierce gales, dense fogs, and occasional ice-bergs until the hold of the ship is filled with salted cod. Strangely enough, these ships are manned not by sailors of English, French, or Scots origin but by the descendants of the Germans who came out from the Palatinate nearly two hundred years ago. They, to-day, most truly carry on the seafaring tradition of the Maritimes.

The huge forests that once covered Nova Scotia and New Brunswick are nearly half gone. Lumbering is now confined largely to New Brunswick. There, the logs, guided by alert and agile river drivers, are floated down the rivers to the saw and pulp mills to be converted into boards, laths, shingles, and pulpwood.

In addition to the industries already mentioned, Nova Scotia has rather extensive coal deposits. Even in the days when the French were at Louisburg, Cape Breton Island was known for its coal mines. Later, other rich veins were found in Pictou and Cumberland counties along the Northumberland Strait. Many New England fishermen, on their way home from the Grand Banks, stopped off to get a few tons of coal when they could evade their adversaries the French. Some of the coal seams in Cape Breton run far out under the ocean, and many miners make their way each day to their appointed stations beneath the bottom of the sea. Steel and coal are the basis of industry and the source of much of Nova Scotia's wealth. Iron ore is shipped in to Sydney from near-by Newfoundland to be processed in furnaces.

Although their are many towns in the Maritimes, few can be classed as cities. Halifax, though small by comparison with Montreal or Toronto, is by far the largest and most cosmopolitan. Many of the early buildings are gone, yet the streets seem to retain a flavor of the past. The old, grey fortifications on Citadel Hill, built nearly two hundred years ago to defy the French at Louisburg, still brood over the city. Today, the Brunswick Street barracks, the salute of the guns on Citadel Hill, and the playing of military bands recall the former pomp of gold lace and plumed hats, of military governors and full-dress regiments.

CHAPTER IV

◇◇ *Central Canada—Quebec and Ontario* ◇◇

The two giant provinces of central Canada are about one third the size of the United States. Ontario alone is almost twice as large as Texas. Together these two provinces comprise over a quarter of Canada's area and include sixty per cent of its population. They touch the United States, and at the same time, reach out toward the Arctic wastes. In the south, agriculture and industries abound and many of their people enjoy a high standard of living, while along the northern shores of Quebec the Eskimo obtains much of his food and clothing from the mammals of the sea.

The Ottawa River forms a part of the boundary between the two provinces. East of the boundary, French traditions, language, and customs dominate; west of it, those of England prevail. The early French settlers made their homes along the St. Lawrence and its tributaries. Most of the English, when they arrived, moved west of the French communities, to settle along Lake Ontario. In the intervening years, the growing population has occupied all the available fertile land in the St. Lawrence Valley.

The United States and Canada share four of the Great Lakes. With the building of the famous "Soo" locks at Sault Ste. Marie, the Welland Canal at Niagara, and the St. Lawrence Canals above Montreal it became possible for ships to make the passage from the head of Lake Superior to Montreal.

The soil in the St. Lawrence Valley is excellent; farming is widespread and profitable. This same area, in addition to being intensely agricultural, has become Canada's chief industrial center. For many years industry in central Canada was hampered by a lack of coal deposits. With the development of hydroelectric power, Ontario and Quebec have come into their own—more than into their own, to judge by the dissatisfaction of the other provinces which cannot hope to rival the unbeatable combination of cheap power, a thousand-odd miles of inland waterways, and over half of the consumer market located on their own doorstep.

Northern Ontario and Quebec until recent years were largely uninhabited. Cold, forbidding, and apparently unfertile—settlers in search of farm lands turned westward to the Prairies. Unfertile and bleak they may have appeared, but their fertility was to respond to the divining rod of the prospector rather than to the spade of the farmer. This mighty ledge of rock, lying within the Canadian Shield and broken by countless lakes and streams, has been found to contain some of the most valuable mineral deposits in the world. Much of it is still untapped, even unexplored, and already it has yielded millions in wealth.

Quebec is the home of the French Canadians. On a rocky promontory jutting out into the St. Lawrence, Champlain built the settlement which he called by that name. The early French settlers have multiplied to three and a half million and, in addition, two million have overflowed into the United States. Succeeding generations have lived on through changes of government, much as their forefathers lived, singularly aloof from the influence of the outside world, their lives revolving about their farms, their families, and their church.

The ideal approach to the city of Quebec is by water. Entering the St. Lawrence from the ocean, one sails for miles up an ever-narrowing stream. At first the shoreline is indistinct along the distant horizon. To the south lies the Gaspé Peninsula where the Appalachian Mountains meet the sea and where a road along the edge of the cliffs provides the traveller with memories for a lifetime. Life is hard and austere in the fishing villages with their little white houses and grey fishing huts. Their food and clothing consist largely of what they can provide for themselves. Until recently they have had little contact with the outside world. It required the curiosity of the untiring American tourist to discover the incomparable charm of this isolated spot.

As one moves up the river the northern shoreline appears as a vast sweep of forest extending to the water's edge. The Saguenay River, coming down, deep and black, from the north, makes a visible line as it joins with the green of the St. Lawrence. If we were to sail up the Saguenay, which by the way is another favorite vacation spot for Americans, we would pass into a realm of almost matchless beauty. For miles the river runs wide, deep, and black, through a canyon. Evergreen cliffs tower on either side, rising higher and still higher, until we come to Capes Trinity and Eternity, two mighty outcroppings of rock which guard the entrance to Eternity Bay.

But we must on to the city of Quebec. Past Murray Bay and Baie St. Paul, we find ourselves approaching Isle d'Orleans. (Jacques Cartier called it the Isle of Bacchus, when he found it laden with wild grapes.) Isle d'Orleans provides one of the best examples of early rural life—beautiful French farmhouses with their steep, black roofs and whitewashed faces, wayside shrines, and lovely churches whose wood carvings have become widely known and commended in the world of art.

Just above Isle d'Orleans sits Quebec, a giant rock dominating the landscape. The grey, cold walls of its fortifications merge with the steeples and towers of the town. What tales those walls and cliffs could tell! Under the shadow of the cliff, on a rim of low-land bordering the river's edge, Champlain erected the first settlement. Known as Lower Town, it is today a crowded mass of wharves, narrow streets, and grey stone buildings with their Norman roofs and chimneys.

Quebec is the only walled city of North America. Though their days of usefulness have passed, the walls have been repaired and they blend with the Norman roofs and gables to give unity to the town. It is also the mother city of the Roman Catholic

Church in Canada. Clergy are everywhere, parish priests, exalted dignitaries, teaching brethren and sisters—a medley of black and brown and grey, with occasionally a touch of white.

The Ursuline Convent, established three hundred years ago by Mère Marie, is still instructing its children in the ways of faith and truth. Indians have threatened its existence, fires have ravished its walls, and the fury of battle has echoed around it, but still the Order continues on the same site, with the same garden. To that garden Montcalm was carried when he fell mortally wounded in his struggle with Wolfe. Under its walls he lies buried, laid to rest by faithful nuns, among them Soeur Esther Marie Joseph.

Soeur Esther Marie once lived as a little Puritan maid in Wells, Maine. Her grandfather was the Reverend John Wheelwright, a Puritan minister, and she was christened Esther Wheelwright. Indians raided Wells one night and little Esther was captured. Her parents never saw her again. Years later, she was brought to Quebec where she entered the Ursuline Convent. When she grew up, she joined the Order and eventually became its Mother Superior.

On summer evenings the town goes walking on Dufferin Terrace. High above the Lower Town, along the edge of the rock, the Château Frontenac behind and the river below, the people promenade back and forth—families, elderly couples, young men in groups, and girls chattering together. One rarely hears English spoken for over ninety per cent of the city is French. The sunset guns from the citadel mark the close of day, and soon the terrace becomes quiet as people move off toward home.

The shoreline between Quebec and Montreal is thickly settled. Farms and villages showing white against the green and gold of the fields, together with massive churches towering skyward, testify to an abiding faith in God and husbandry. Wayside shrines are an important part of the Quebec landscape—for this is a devout countryside. Some are little more than humble crosses set in a field, others are more elaborately executed. Ste. Anne de Beaupré and the Basilica of St. Joseph in Montreal have become noted throughout North America for the miraculous cures which have occurred within their walls, and thousands of pilgrims journey each year to pray before their altars.

Montreal, Canada's great metropolis, is located on an island at the junction of the Ottawa and the St. Lawrence rivers. Though more than half the people are French, Montreal bears the imprint of the twentieth century. Unlike Quebec, which seems unmoved by the confusion of the modern world, Montreal is very much the active business city and a center of commerce, shipping, industry, and finance. A sizeable population of English-speaking people live in the western part of the city; the large retail stores are English; and that language is much more widely used than elsewhere in the province. Although its busy streets are lined with modern office buildings, large department stores, and handsome hotels, no one could possibly mistake Montreal for an American city.

The cross on the top of Mount Royal, illuminated by night, commemorates that earlier cross planted by Cartier on his visit to Montreal in 1534. The mountain looks smaller today than it did to Cartier four hundred years ago because the city has encircled it and has grown halfway up its sides. Horse-drawn carriages, or *calèches,* clop clop through the streets to show visitors the sights of the city, through the grounds of McGill University, past the homes of the former fur barons of the North West Company, to the top of the mountain. From the lookout one can see far to left and right. Immediately below are the homes and estates of prosperous Montrealers, sumptuous residences built into the hillside, each commanding a view only slightly less extensive than that from the mountaintop. The great dome of the Basilica of St. Joseph and the towers of the University of Montreal rise above the trees on the north side of the mountain. The Green Mountains of Vermont and the Adirondacks of New York outline the southern horizon. The shoreline is a crowded confusion of industrial plants, grain elevators, and railway yards. Grain from the prairies, minerals from the northland, and manufactured goods from other parts of the Dominion pour in and out again to the markets of the world. Montreal is the terminus for both the Great Lakes steamers and the ocean-going liners, the world's greatest inland port.

North of Quebec and Montreal the land soon rises to become the Laurentian Mountains, the southern boundary of the Canadian Shield. Their southern slopes have become a popular year-round vacationland. In winter skiers flash down their slopes, and in summer vacationers crowd their picturesque hotels and chalets for bathing, hiking, fishing, and other sports. Autumn finds travellers weaving around the hillsides and through the French villages to enjoy the brilliant foliage.

Farther north, beyond the line of the old settlements, the wooded Laurentian highlands resound with the echo of the woodsman's axe as the great trees are felled to feed the pulp and paper mills along the rivers. Nowhere else are pulp and paper mills so big as those on the Ottawa, the St. Maurice, and the Saguenay rivers, for electric power is cheap and abundant.

Only within the past few decades have the mineral possibilities of Quebec been realized, and even yet many regions of its northland have not been explored. For many years Thetford and the surrounding vicinity have supplied eighty per cent of the world's output of asbestos. The Noranda gold-silver-copper mines at Rouyn near the Ottawa River are well developed. Prospectors are still at work, new mines are being opened constantly, and northern towns seem to grow up over night.

Water power is Quebec's greatest natural resource. It runs the pulp and paper mills, the mines, the chemical and textile industries. With the outbreak of the war, the United Nations needed aluminium in quantities far greater than their present industries could supply. Plans were soon underway to enlarge the aluminium company already established on the Saguenay. The power plants then in operation were inadequate. In 1941 construction of a new power plant began. In spite of the rigorous winters, work progressed all year round. With temperatures from forty to fifty below zero, men could work only a short time before being relieved. No mention of this stupendous project reached the public ear until it was formally announced by the Canadian government early in 1943. Before the end of that year Shipshaw, one of the biggest power developments on the continent, was completed and the Aluminium Company of Canada, in near-by Arvida, expanded to become the largest plant of its kind in the world.

It would be difficult to find a sight more unusual and astonishing than that of Shipshaw and Arvida—in the midst of the forests of Quebec, seventy-five miles up the Saguenay River. Arvida is a model town built for the employees of the company—a fairy tale come to life. Wide streets are bordered by luxuriant masses of blossoms and shrubbery. Houses, freshly painted, are attractive and well spaced, each with lawn and flower garden. The shopping center and the hotel are second to none in the Dominion. A few miles away the forest is broken once more by the powerhouse and giant spillway of Shipshaw. Once again beauty goes hand in hand with efficiency. The road sweeps around curves to disclose a hillside carpeted with flowers, and great masses of concrete, all in a frame of evergreen.

Ontario spans four of the Great Lakes on her southern border and reaches northward to Hudson Bay. Into this region the majority of Loyalists moved as they fled to safety through New York or New Hampshire. The first to arrive settled along the St. Lawrence in its upper reaches, just beyond the French communities. Later settlers moved farther west into the Niagara Peninsula. A line drawn from the southern part of Georgian Bay to the city of Ottawa more or less divides southern from northern Ontario. South of this line is Old Ontario, the home of the great majority of the population; north of it lie the forested rocks of the Canadian Shield.

If we enter Ontario by the St. Lawrence, the ship passes through a series of canals. The river drops some two hundred feet between Lake Ontario and Montreal. In some places it is calm and peaceful as in Lac St. François; in others it curves and winds downward with a furious roar. Before building the canals, the river was not navigable beyond Montreal and long, difficult portages were necessary to reach Lake Ontario. The French voyageurs, on their way to the fur-trading posts of the West, preferred to travel via the Ottawa River and Ontario's inland lakes to Georgian Bay.

Finally we come within sight of the Thousand Islands. Some are large and green and fertile, housing castles or comfortable homes, others mere rocks jutting out of the stream. Kingston appears in sight, very grey and old. Like Quebec it has an unchanged and unchanging quality. The memory of history seems very real. In the seventeenth century, Frontenac, and later La Salle, built forts here. The War of 1812 brought an American fleet to its shores, for it was then a garrison town. For a time it became the temporary seat of government for Upper and Lower Canada (later Ontario and Quebec). From wars and government it turned to the pursuit of education, to become the home of Queen's University and of the Royal Military College, Canada's West Point.

Lake Ontario presents a scene of great activity—lake steamers bound for Montreal with cargoes of grain, ferries running between Coburg and Rochester, New York, fishing vessels out for the day's catch to replenish the city markets. As we approach the western end of the lake our goal is Toronto, Canada's second largest city and the provincial capital. Her harbor, sheltered behind an island, is impressive. A lot of money has been spent on landscaping the waterfront, and the results are very rewarding.

Toronto is a modern American city, with wide streets, excellent stores, scores of industries, beautiful parks and tree-shaded residential sections. Its people point with pride to the Canadian

Bank of Commerce Building and to the Royal York Hotel; one, the highest building, the other, the largest hotel in the British Empire. Toronto businessmen look forward to the day when the St. Lawrence Waterway plan for deepening and widening the river—if it ever materializes—will make their city a great port for ocean vessels. Montreal, on the other hand, views such a project with alarm for it will take commerce beyond her docks into the Great Lakes.

In addition to being a commercial and industrial city, Toronto is widely recognized throughout Canada as a center of art and music. The University of Toronto, reputed to be the largest university in the British Empire, has an exceptionally fine campus. One building in particular, University College, is considered to be one of the best examples of Romanesque architecture on the North American continent.

It would be difficult to find two cities in one country so unlike each other as Toronto and Montreal, and yet they are only a few hundred miles apart. Montreal is a mass of mellow, grey stone buildings climbing up the mountainside; the skyline is broken by scores of spires surmounted by a Roman cross. On nearly every street an austere convent or seminary stands aloof behind its high wall. Many of the imposing buildings are connected in one way or another with the Roman Catholic Church. French is the prevailing tongue and all public notices are printed in two languages.

Toronto, on the other hand, is as flat as any city in the United States Middle West. Miles of its streets are lined with substantial, red brick homes, set closely together. The largest and most prosperous churches are generally Protestant, and if one were to ask a question in French it would provoke an expression of astonishment if not disdain.

Stemming out from Toronto, east, north, and west, railways and highways connect the industrial cities of the southern peninsula —for it is in Toronto and the surrounding cities that the greatest concentration of manufacturing is found. Toronto alone contains more manufacturing establishments than any other Canadian city. The reason for Ontario's success is that her people developed resources which geography and Nature placed at their disposal. Industry produced more industry. She is well placed to distribute goods eastward and westward by both land and water. She has an abundance of cheap power from Niagara and a multitude of inland lakes and rivers; and, in addition, Canada's most concentrated consumer market within a two-hundred mile radius of Toronto.

Between the cities, and especially north of Lake Erie, agriculture is very important. Some areas are given over almost entirely to raising cattle either for beef or for dairy products. In other sections, grapes, peaches, apples, or tobacco provide the farmer's income.

Ottawa began life under the name of Bytown and, like Hull, its neighbor across the river, had its origin in lumber. It has risen in the world to become the capital of the nation and more menial pursuits have been put aside in the interests of the major task at hand, that of guiding the destiny of nearly twelve million people.

All roads seem to lead to Parliament Hill. Its grey, Gothic buildings, arranged about a quadrangle on the heights, dominate the scene. To the right, the Château Laurier, replete with Norman turrets and a moat-like canal completes the landscape. Parliament Hill, to the casual observer, is a handsome, commanding sight. But it is more than that! It is a solemn sight. Those massive, stone buildings stand as a tangible memorial to the democratic way of life, to the essential dignity of the common man. The Peace Tower peals forth its carillon, that all who hear may be reminded of Canada's World War dead.

The city itself is one of exceptional beauty. A system of driveways winds for miles through the town, flanked by parks, gardens, and beautiful homes on one side, and by the canal or miniature lakes on the other. Ottawa stands at the junction of three rivers. The Gatineau from the mountains to the north, the Rideau from the south, and the Ottawa from the west come together in the Chaudière Cataract. This cataract, once the object of Indian veneration and ceremony, are lost today in a confusion of pulp and saw mills which use their power.

The Muskoka Lakes, Georgian Bay District, Algonquin Park, and Lake Nipissing, named by Champlain, are thronged in summer with pleasure seekers. North Bay is the gateway to the mines of northern Ontario, and an active center for the summer tourist trade. In recent years its popularity has been somewhat eclipsed as Callender drew thousands of curious sightseers to visit the Dionne quintuplets.

North and west of North Bay is the region which contains such mining towns as Sudbury, Coppercliff, Cobalt, Kirkland Lake, and Timmins—each the setting for stories of fabulous wealth. The riches of the Canadian Shield were first discovered in Ontario, quite by accident. When the Canadian Pacific Railway was being built, copper was unearthed in the middle of the wilderness north of Georgian Bay. Prospectors followed to discover tremendous copper-nickel deposits, and Sudbury became the center of the world's nickel industry. Kirkland Lake and Timmins are but two of many prosperous cities built on gold. The discovery of silver led to the settlement of Cobalt. In the early 1900's it became the most noted silver town in the world as nuggets of almost pure silver weighing several hundred pounds were taken from the earth.

The last link in the Trans-Canada Highway has recently been completed and the next few years may see great changes in the region north of Lake Superior. At present, settlement is scattered except at either end of the lake. Massive grain elevators at Fort William and Port Arthur, Canada's twin cities, handle the grain of the prairies destined for Europe. Sault Ste. Marie, between Superior and Huron, provides safe passage for lake boats.

CHAPTER V

❧ *The Prairie Provinces* ❧

Manitoba, Saskatchewan, and Alberta, the provinces of the Canadian prairies, are a part of the Great Plains region extending northward from the Gulf of Mexico. Like the United States Middle West, this region has specialized in farming. Most of the Canadian people depend indirectly, as well as directly, on the wheat farmer of the prairies. He feeds them, and sells his surplus to other nations. When he can sell his wheat at good prices, he buys liberally. Industries boom, people are employed, and everybody eats well. If his crop fails, or brings a low price, he not only suffers, but the whole country with him. Because he cannot buy, the manufacturer produces fewer goods and discharges some of his help. Men are out of jobs and there are fewer pay envelopes, so they stop buying and many people are hungry and discontented. Because the prairies export more wheat than any other similar area in the world, low prices or crop failures bring tragedy.

Most people picture the prairies as flat with perhaps an occasional lone tree here and there. They think of fields, yellow with waving grain, stretching for miles out to the horizon. While the land looks level, much of it is also rolling and sometimes hilly. The surface of the prairies has a definite slope from the Rocky Mountains eastward. This slope is broken into three levels or steppes. Each is on a higher level, and separated from the other by a range of hills. The river valleys, when they appear, are a surprise. They are invisible from a distance because the water has cut deep canyons, or coulees, into the soft soil. Some of the canyons have water flowing through them, others are merely the dried-out remains of former rivers. Wherever there is water, trees grow in groves and clusters.

The rich, black soil of Manitoba, which provides wealth to many people, has a strange history. Many years ago a big icecap around Hudson Bay dammed back the water to make southern Manitoba a giant lake. Lake Agassiz, as it is called, went southward through the Red River, on into the Mississippi, and out to sea. The Assiniboine River, then turbulent and muddy, each year deposited mud on the bottom of Lake Agassiz. As the icecap around Hudson Bay melted, most of the water in the lake was drawn off, and left behind a thick layer of fine sediment. Lakes Winnipeg, Winnipegosis, and Manitoba are all that remain of that early lake, once bigger than all the Great Lakes combined.

The "treeless prairie," so called, forms a band across the southern part of the three provinces—only as far north as the lakes in Manitoba, up to Saskatoon in Saskatchewan, and about a hundred miles north of Calgary in Alberta. Just north of the prairie is a semiwooded belt, which when cleared makes good farming land. Above that, the Canadian Shield forms a cap covering a great part of Manitoba, slightly less of Saskatchewan, and northeastern Alberta. As in northern Ontario and Quebec, the land is rather low and generally rocky, broken by irregular valleys and ravines, carpeted with forests, and strewn with a multitude of lakes and rivers. A wealth of minerals lies under its rocky cap, its extent and value still uncertain.

The climate of the Prairies is similar to that of the United States Middle West. Summers are hot, and winters are cold—north of the border they are even colder. November finds everybody well launched into winter. The lakes and rivers freeze over; snow covers the ground; and the temperature drops and drops, to remain well below zero for weeks at a time. At night, the skies sparkle and blaze with Northern Lights. The days are beautiful. The sun shines brightly; snow crunches under foot; the sky is brilliant blue, and the air clear and dry. "What a day to be alive!" you say as you start off briskly down the street. Ten minutes later you wonder if by any chance you have forgotten to put on a few important items of clothing. The sun is still in the sky, bright and sparkling, but without the slightest apparent trace of heat. So, sinking into your clothes, you rush down the street, stopping off on the way, if possible, to thaw out.

Alberta, alone of the Prairie Provinces gets any benefit from the warm Pacific air. When the wind is from the west, it blows through the mountain passes, warm and dry. In five or ten minutes the temperature may rise forty or fifty degrees. These winds, known as the *chinooks,* eat the snow from the earth, absorb most of its moisture, leaving a few nasty puddles on the frozen ground. A little later the snow has vanished and cattle are placidly grazing on the dried bunch grass.

Manitoba began life in 1812 as the Red River Colony. The little settlement in the heart of the fur-trading district was tried, like Job, almost beyond endurance. Man and Nature seemed joined in a conspiracy to oust the pioneers. The métis, French-Indian half-breeds, feared for their future security as trappers if farming became established. The fur traders also saw their livelihood in danger of extinction. Urged on by the latter, the métis attacked the white settlement and drove the people away. The settlers returned, to be attacked again. Grasshoppers stripped their fields; frosts blighted their crops; and the Red River overflowed to flood their cabins. They were almost defeated—but they happened to be Scotsmen, and stubborn. The little colony lingered on, alone and forgotten; the métis living on one side of the river, and the Scotsmen on the other.

Their first road to the outside world connected them with St. Paul, Minnesota. Through the deep forests, the Red River carts jounced and creaked as they slowly made their way to market in Minnesota with a load of produce and, not infrequently, a few fine packs of illegal northern pelts, caught at the expense of the Hudson's Bay Company.

When the settlers of the Red River came to know Americans

and other Canadians, they grew dissatisfied with their lot. As a remote colony under the control of the Hudson's Bay Company, they were isolated from Canada and cut off from civilization by the international boundary. They talked of becoming a British colony, of joining the United States, or of joining Canada. Finally, in the winter of 1856-57 a petition signed by nearly six hundred settlers asked Canada to take over the region. Instead of answering the petition, Canada entered into negotiations with the Hudson's Bay Company. The latter agreed to sell the western lands for £300,000 (about $1,500,000). Although the desired result was achieved, the manner of accomplishing it infuriated both the white settlers and the métis. Neither group had been consulted. They and their land were apparently being transferred from one owner to another. A métis uprising forced the Canadian government to negotiate with the people—a thing it should have done in the first place, considering the petition it had received.

Manitoba was not always its present size. When it joined the Dominion in 1870, it was a small square, crowded down in the southeastern corner, and jokingly described as "the postage stamp province." Between this tiny province and what is now British Columbia stretched the Northwest Territories, fifteen hundred miles of plain and forest, inhabited by Indians, métis, and buffalo. Although a railway to the Pacific was completed in 1885, there could be little hope of settlement in the territories while free homesteads were available in United States and good land remained in eastern Canada. Fortunately for Canada, the United States frontier was declared closed in 1890 and settlers began to turn northward into the prairies.

For Canada this was an opportunity long desired, and not to be missed. The government organized a campaign to attract as many settlers as possible. Through advertisements in the United States and British newspapers, and pamphlets, they proclaimed the advantages which Canada offered. They even brought trainloads of people to see for themselves the wonders so widely heralded. Soon immigrants began pouring into the country. Of the three million settlers to Canada between 1897 and 1914, nearly one third came from the United States, another third from Britain, and the remainder from southern and eastern Europe, the Balkans, Russia, Austria-Hungary, and Germany. The great majority, made their way to the prairies, for the opening of the West was the outstanding event of the early years of the twentieth century. Communities seemed to grow up almost overnight. People who had long lived in the eastern provinces caught the contagion and flocked westward. By 1905 a new form of government was needed in the Northwest Territories, and the land was divided into Saskatchewan and Alberta.

Slightly less than half of the people in the Prairie Provinces are of British origin. A few are métis, descendants of the French voyageurs who years before took Indian wives and settled in the wilderness. The rest have come from Europe in the last fifty years.

Manitoba #1, Hard is king of the wheat world. It commands top prices in all markets, and bakers demand it for their best breads. Wheat farming is a hazardous occupation. Any number of things may destroy a crop between planting and harvest. Too little rain may mean dust storms and the blowing away of the rich top soil, or insufficient moisture for the plants. Too much rain may delay planting in spring, may cause rust in summer, or may prevent harvesting when the wheat is ready. Hail storms may flatten a field in a few minutes. A particularly late spring or early autumn may leave too few days for the wheat to ripen. Because the odds are so great, government scientists studied for years to produce varieties of wheat that would maintain a high standard of quality, produce well, mature quickly, and yet be strong to resist such ills as were likely to strike the growing crops. Marquis wheat proved to be the answer. It combined quality, quantity, and early ripening with resistance to hail and wind.

The prairie farmer must grow a wheat which will ripen early. Frost is likely to come suddenly. The success or failure of a year's work may depend on days, or even hours. When the harvest season arrives, farmers are in their fields from dawn to dark, working feverishly against time. Many of them have turned to combines to aid them in the race against frost.

The average traveller is inclined to judge the prosperity of a farmer by the size and condition of his barns. On the prairies that method of measurement would prove very misleading, for the wheat farmers use barns only to house their horses and machinery. They truck the grain from field to railway siding as part of the harvesting process. Every district has its row of grain elevators on a railway siding. When the farmer arrives with his load of wheat he has it weighed, and then he can have it hoisted by machinery into the elevator, or, if he prefers to save money, he can shovel his own grain into a railway boxcar. Samples of grain are taken from each car and sent to be graded by government experts. The railway cars are sealed; the long freight trains move out; and the wheat is on its way to the markets of the world. Some trains go east to Winnipeg, Montreal, and Europe via the Great Lakes; some go west to Vancouver and the Pacific; and others go north to Churchill on Hudson Bay for shipment to Liverpool.

The uncertainty of the wheat market has driven many prairie farmers to produce other crops—less romantic but more practical from an economic point of view. A number of them have turned to mixed farming. Oats, barley, flax, sugar beets, and vegetables grow very well. In recent years there has been a growing movement from worn-out farms of the South toward the Peace River district of northern Alberta and British Columbia. Although extensive farming had never before been attempted so far north, the long summer days, together with the rich soil, seem to make up for the short season.

Alberta contains many large ranches, among them, *High River* owned by the Duke of Windsor. Livestock and beef cattle thrive especially well on the bunch grass that grows on the foothills of the Rocky Mountains. They eat it all the year round, for it makes excellent fodder. Even in winter they are able to stay on the ranges, thanks to the chinook winds which absorb the snow.

For years Manitoba and Saskatchewan depended upon wheat for their prosperity, while the mineral wealth of the north lay idle. Although mining is not by any means fully developed, they are now producing copper, zinc, lead, and gold in quantity. Some years ago the discovery of fabulous seams of pitchblende and gold north of Saskatchewan and Alberta sent prospectors hurrying to the region around Lake Athabaska.

Alberta has extensive coal deposits. Fur traders heard of the "burning rocks" from the Indians, and used them to heat their trading posts. Today, Alberta's mines lead the Dominion in the production of coal. In addition, valuable wells of natural gas and petroleum are located in the Turner Valley, southwest of Calgary.

Calgary, within sight of the Rocky Mountains, in the midst of the ranching country, was once famous as a cattle town. Fifty years ago, cowboys galloped through its streets. Although the "Wild West" is no longer really wild, each year cowboys and Indians gather to re-enact a drama of early days. The first part of July finds thousands of people from western Canada and the United States converging on the city for the famous Calgary Stampede. A parade, resplendent with color, formally opens the week's celebrations. Mounted Police in full dress, dignitaries from the federal and provincial governments, Indians in war bonnet and buckskin followed by their squaws and papooses, army regiments, cowboys, bagpipes, floats, regimental bands, Red River carts and prairie schooners—the history of the West moves on.

For a week the fair grounds are crowded with spectators. Cowboys from as far away as Texas compete with each other in all sorts of impossible events. Some enter the wild-steer decorating contest, where the aim is to reach one of the steers as they gallop madly up the field, dismount, and place a red ribbon on one of the horns. Others, in teams of two, compete in the wild-cow milking contest. One, on horseback, lassoes a cow and holds her by a rope around the neck, while the other, entangled in a wild thrashing of rear end, endeavors to get milk into a quart bottle. And so it goes throughout the week, wild-horse riding, wild-steer riding, wild-calf roping, and chuck-wagon races—a succession of incredible events, all blood-and-thunder drama. For this is no imitation show; the horses, the steers, and the calves are really wild. The air resounds with thunder of hoofs, shrieks of terror, or cheers of applause. Cowboys enter the arena in brilliant satin shirts, frequently to emerge torn and tattered.

Although most of the mountains are in British Columbia, the Rockies begin in Alberta, within sight of Calgary. Two of the earliest and most beautiful of Canada's national parks, Banff and Jasper, are located on those eastern slopes. Encircled by massive mountain ranges, carpeted alternately by ice-fields and sheltered Alpine valleys, and studded with brilliantly blue glacier-fed lakes, Banff and Jasper provide a continuous wild-life sanctuary, and an incomparable vacation resort.

Scattered throughout the prairies a number of cities serve as manufacturing and distributing centers for the surrounding countryside. Winnipeg has outdistanced all other western cities except Vancouver. Formerly the site of the little Red River colony, for many years known as Fort Garry of the Hudson's Bay Company, Winnipeg is the capital of Manitoba, the chief city of the prairies, the Chicago of Canada, and the wheat center of the world. A traveller arriving in Winnipeg is always impressed by its spaciousness and especially by the width of its main street. Ideal from the standpoint of the motorist, it poses a major problem to an individual whose destination demands a crossing on foot. All trains east and west pass through her freight yards. From late summer onward wheat pours into Winnipeg to be graded and shipped out again. Freight trains from the West are arriving constantly and railroad yards are crowded with cars. Some are full of wheat, others waiting to be filled and on their way to Fort William and Port Arthur before winter comes to the Great Lakes.

CHAPTER VI

❖❖ *British Columbia* ❖❖

Sʜᴜᴛ ᴏꜰꜰ from the rest of Canada by the barrier of mountains, British Columbia looks out on the Pacific. No other part of Canada, indeed few places on earth, can rival the splendor of her mountains. Nature here is fierce and elemental, with jagged, glacier-capped crags, raging mountain torrents, deep forest-clad canyons, or long winding inlets. The Continental Divide, the roof of the continent, forms the boundary between British Columbia and Alberta. Down either side mountain streams rush eastward and westward; the former to find their way, after several thousand miles, to the Arctic Ocean or Hudson Bay; the latter to wind through canyons and mingle at last with the waters of the Pacific.

The mountains known to us as "the Rockies," bear, in the language of the geographer, the impressive label of the Cordilleran System. At first glance, a map of British Columbia presents a very confusing and discouraging impression. Mountains seem to be everywhere, in complete disorder. Gradually a pattern emerges. Four chief ranges run from northwest to southeast more or less parallel to the coast. Between the ranges are a series of valleys, or trenches, ploughed out many years ago by the melting of the immense glaciers as they moved south. The Coast Mountains and the St. Elias Mountains are on the Pacific side, the Selkirks and the Rockies on the east. The remains of a former range, now nearly submerged and surrounded by the ocean, shows up in the tangle of islands stretching downward from Alaska.

British Columbia offers climate to suit any taste. The people of her coastal area and Vancouver Island enjoy moderate temperatures all the year round. The rainfall is heavy especially in winter, gardens are luxuriant, flowers begin to blossom in February and March, and the western slopes of the Coast Range abound in giant timber. Just east of the first mountain range, rain seldom falls, bright sunlight floods the valleys week after week, and the air is dry. Summer is much, much warmer, but winter is correspondingly cold. The rain of the coast becomes snow on the slopes of the inland mountains—sometimes as much as a hundred feet a year! In contrast with the luxuriant vegetation near the ocean, the land is frequently parched for want of rain. Scrub and a scattering of stunted trees cover the mountains. Summer is usually cool in the mountains, and heavy clothes are not at all uncomfortable. In some places, skiers sweep down snowy slopes or mountain climbers explore age-old glaciers, while far below on the same hillside bathers seek relief from the summer heat.

British Columbia's first settlers were fur traders who penetrated farther and farther westward in search of precious pelts. South of the border, the land swarmed with homesteaders, while for years to the north, the Hudson's Bay Company reigned supreme.

The cry of "gold" went out from the Fraser River Valley in 1858. Prospectors in California left their claims to rush northward, sailors deserted their ships, and farmers their crops. Boats of all sorts and conditions arrived almost daily to disgorge their human cargo. Young and old, saint and sinner, converged on the Fraser River. Some drowned in the whirlpools and rapids, some nearly starved to death, a few struck it rich, but more lost what little they had. In spite of the odds, thousands were soon on their knees washing the sands for gold. With luck some might make a hundred, even two hundred dollars a day, the majority did well to find the equivalent of ten or twenty dollars.

Fabulous tales of "$1,500 a week," "a quarter of a million in a few months," "a nugget worth $10,000," sent people in a mad scramble farther and farther up the river. As prospectors raced each other up the trackless canyon, supplies had to follow or they would soon have faced starvation. Mule packs served as a temporary expedient, but an all-weather road, wide and smooth enough to bear heavy wagons, was needed. Today, the construction of a road along the edge of the treacherous canyon and down through its deep ravines would bring cheers and applause to its engineers. Remember the Alaska Highway of a few years ago! Eighty years ago such an undertaking was really colossal, and it was completed, four hundred miles of it—the Old Cariboo Road. Chinese coolies were brought in to do the labor, and they remained afterward to pan for gold, in the worn-out areas already largely deserted by the white man.

Back and forth across the face of British Columbia travelled the gold seekers as each new find was proclaimed—to the Cariboo, the Kootenay, the Columbia River. When the stream beds were worked out, the miners dug into the hillsides with picks and shovels. Towns cropped up like mushrooms, peopled with all sorts and conditions of men—united in the one occupation of obtaining easy money. Prosperous miners, boastful of their success, paid well for their wants.

The gold rush lasted about twenty years. As the surface gold was exhausted and rock mining became necessary, the day of the independent miner drew to a close and that of the industrialist dawned. Mining is still an important industry for the people of British Columbia. Gold is still taken from its rocky hillsides in considerable quantities, as are silver, lead, copper, zinc, and coal.

The gold rush, which provided British Columbia with a population almost overnight, provided the British government with the problem of maintaining order among a group notoriously lawless. California offered an excellent example of how not to manage a mining population, and Britain, profiting by that lesson, provided a government which demanded respect—and got it. The people were not satisfied with their newly organized government for long. They found it costly. The Cariboo Road had put them deeply into debt. Gold was becoming scarcer. Some urged that British Columbia join the United States, but more preferred

Canada. Canada won, and British Columbia joined the Dominion as the sixth province in 1871.

The people of British Columbia are very largely English Canadians with small minorities of the other European races, and some forty thousand Asiatics. The Chinese, as we know, were brought in to build the Cariboo Road. They were followed by the Japanese and some Hindus from India. At first, when their numbers were few, they offered a cheap labor supply. As they grew more numerous, hostility developed. Outbreaks similar to those in California occurred, and equally repressive measures were taken to exclude further immigration. With the outbreak of war, Canada, like the United States, interned the Japanese living on her West Coast.

Although agriculture has never been as important to British Columbia as were its forests or its minerals, farming began on a small scale as far back as the gold rush. The need of food for the rapidly growing population was serious. Transportation was slow and uncertain. Prices for the simplest foodstuffs were fantastic. Some of the more prudent who came to find gold, realized that money could be made from wheat, vegetables, and meat, so they settled down to farming, secure in the certainty that there was more than one way to get a share of the "gold dust."

The farmers of British Columbia are of three kinds, some do mixed farming, some raise cattle, and some are fruit farmers. Suitable farm land is quite limited. The coastal area was the first to be developed. With the aid of irrigation, the interior river valleys were made to produce well. The bunch grass growing on the higher levels between the mountain ranges provides excellent year-round fodder. As in Alberta, the chinook winds make it possible for cattle to feed on the dried grass all winter. Two valleys in particular, the Okanagan and the Columbia-Kootenay, have developed sizeable fruit-raising areas, picturesque in their setting around the lakes and streams, and practical in the competition they offer the Annapolis Valley and the Niagara Peninsula.

Halibut, cod, herring, pilchard, numerous types and varieties of fish, crowd her coastal bays and inlets to make British Columbia a fisherman's paradise. But the salmon taken from her shores, and especially from the Fraser River, form her largest and proudest catch. Each spring the river comes alive. Hoards of salmon crowd up the river to reach the pools in which they were born four years before. They fight their way for miles up the swiftly moving stream, battering themselves against the rocks, leaping over waterfalls or rapids, until they at last arrive, exhausted, at the little pool in which they were hatched, to lay their eggs and die. Indians spear their salmon from the river bank, but the white man has made salmon fishing into "big business." The fish are caught in nets and are rushed to one of the scores of canneries along the coast. There they are mechanically processed to emerge canned, labelled, and ready for shipment.

Since early days the forests of British Columbia have provided wealth for its people. Year after year lumber brings in the largest part of their income. The Douglas fir of British Columbia is rivalled only by California's redwoods in height and girth. It frequently grows upward for one hundred feet before putting out any branches. Other types of trees—spruces, hemlocks, cedars—are marketed, but the Douglas fir is in constant demand.

Life for the logger, many miles from civilization and deep in the woods, is hard and lonely. The buildings around which his world revolves are long, squat, and uninviting. Built to be used for only a few seasons, they are made as cheaply as possible. Rough boards provide the floor, ceiling, and walls. Tar paper slapped on the outside, keeps out the worst of the weather. A few big box stoves, long, rough, board tables, and double-decker bunks provide most of the living equipment. The air reeks with smoke and the heat is suffocating. A good logger must be hardy, skillful, and well fed. One of his chief pleasures seems to be eating—prodigious quantities of food. The cook is by far the most popular person in camp.

Most logging areas in Canada depend on near-by rivers to carry their logs to the sawmills. British Columbia has many rivers and streams, but they are too swift moving to be useful for lumbering. So donkey engines are used to drag or carry the logs to the water's edge where they can be bound into rafts to be towed by tugs to the sawmill. There, a perpetual stream of giant logs is fed into a monstrous machine which squares them, then simultaneously, by means of a series of parallel band saws, cuts each log into long boards.

The tourist trade provides a large part of British Columbia's peacetime income. Thousands of people travel from the United States and across Canada to gaze on the majestic wonders of her mountains, lakes, and rivers. A trip through the Canadian Rockies is considered by many to be in a class with a trip to London or Paris, a part of one's education! Large areas of British Columbia and Alberta are set aside as national parks, where deer and moose roam at will and where the traveller can live in princely splendour, or in more modest fashion. Yoho, with its Kicking Horse Pass and O'Hara Lake, is the great Alpine climbing center; Kootenay, the park of the red-walled canyons; Mount Revelstoke, the favorite for winter sports; and Glacier, the home of Illicillewaet, the giant glacier.

The way to see and know the Rocky Mountains is to live with them, to camp on their forested slopes, to fish in their deep pools and lakes. Roads have been built through the parks. If you must motor, let someone else take the wheel, for the tortuous curves demand the undivided attention of the driver. The Canadian National and the Canadian Pacific Railways pass through some of the finest parts of the mountains, over narrow trestles several hundred feet high, around curves that leave one gasping, and occasionally through tunnels. Observation cars, both closed and open, make it possible to see up, down, and around. Before the war, trains stopped at special beauty spots while passengers enjoyed waterfalls and glaciers at their leisure.

The Rockies by air are incomparable. In clear weather planes fly within a few thousand feet of the mountain peaks, and below one looks into the ranges spread out in a giant relief map, their huge yawning jaws, jagged and sharp and horrible.

Victoria, on Vancouver Island, is the provincial capital, and the most "English" spot in Canada. Chiefly residential, it contains a number of retired British military men and other government officials who, clad in the inevitable tweeds, take their brisk, daily constitutional accompanied by cane or dog. Life seems leisurely and pleasant. The city has a well-kept, precise air, with few ragged edges. Lawns, hedgerows, and shrubbery are tended with care. Flowers bloom in profusion—orderly profusion. The mild moist winds of the Pacific give Victoria a moderate climate, even in winter. Homes require heat for only a short season, and early in February, long before life comes to the gardens of the East, her lawns and parks are ablaze with spring color.

Vancouver, with about 400,000 population, is little more than fifty years old. In the half century since it has come into existence, it has shot ahead to surpass every other Canadian city except Montreal and Toronto. From its docks, steamers sail for Alaska, Australia, the Orient, and for Europe by way of the Panama Canal. Its mighty grain elevators rival those of Montreal. In the manufacture of lumber it has no rival.

The city presents a striking impression to the traveller arriving by water. At one moment, the beautiful passage, known as the Narrows, is a forest of trees rising high on both sides of the water, then without warning it widens to become an inland harbor, with Vancouver on the right, and on the left, across the harbor, the mountains of the Coast Range rising out of the water. Its harbor teems with activity, great lumber ships are being loaded, grain elevators are pouring out their golden stream, passengers are embarking for New Zealand and the South Pacific.

CHAPTER VII

⋄⋄ *The Northland* ⋄⋄

FROM THE SIXTIETH PARALLEL of latitude northward through the islands of the Arctic Ocean, and from Alaska to Greenland, Canada's Northland spreads over land and sea, an empire in area, a small city in terms of people. It is a land of short, brilliant summers and long, frigid winters; a land where the sun never sets, and where it never rises; a land where man is at the mercy of Nature.

From September to May the earth and sea are buried under a thick blanket of snow and stillness, broken only by the fury of wind and blizzard. People travel by dog sled, and wear several layers of fur to keep them warm. Spring comes suddenly, with little warning. Great rifts appear in the ice. The rocks show through the snow. Soon the reindeer moss is green. Hardy, flowering plants show signs of color, and the scrubby trees put out leaves. The wild ducks, the snow birds, and the geese have arrived for the summer. Nights shorten and days lengthen. June brings the sun to stay for twenty-four hours each day. People rest very little, for it is difficult to sleep. Long after folks in the South have gone to bed, they play games, visit, and have a midnight meal.

Sudden squalls and biting winds in August herald the approach of winter. Snow begins to fall during September. The temperature sinks lower and lower every day. The sea freezes over to remain frozen until the following June. Blizzards rage and the wind sweeps great mountains of snow about, changing the face of the landscape from hour to hour. To venture outside in the face of the raging wind would be folly. You cannot stand upright against its force. The lashing snow cuts the skin and penetrates any openings in the clothing. Outside activity is suspended for a few weeks until the snow has settled and become hardened.

When a crust forms on the snow the dogs are harnessed and made ready, for land and sea have become an icy highway to connect far-distant communities. In the heavens the stars flash with a brilliance unequalled in southern latitudes. Nature's fireworks, the Northern Lights, flare and shoot across the sky—rose red, gold, green and white, in a flood of color.

High up in the lonely outposts of the Arctic live the men who form the backbone of the Hudson's Bay Company, with only the Eskimos or Indian trappers, some government weathermen, and an occasional officer of the Royal Canadian Mounted Police for company. In two's or three's these men live the year round, their only contact with the outside world, an annual ship. It arrives in July, stops for a day to unload a year's provisions, takes on a cargo of furs, and moves off to the next outpost. Naturally, the arrival of the steamer is the big event of the year. The Eskimos gather in advance, pitch tents on the rocky hillsides, and prepare for the gala occasion. Dressed in their best they are ready long before the ship is due to arrive. As soon as the anchor is dropped, they clambor on board for the inevitable meal of tea and biscuits; only after that are they ready for the day's labors.

To the white man, the arrival of the annual ship often means the first outside companionship since last summer, the anticipation of long-delayed Christmas presents, a year's supply of mail and newspapers—to be hoarded and enjoyed until the following July. A winter mail service has been introduced in recent years. It provides variety and a break in the usual daily routine. Mail is flown to one of the posts nearer civilization. There, a member of the Hudson's Bay Company carries it by dog sled to the next post, accompanied by the indispensable Eskimo guide. This usually means a journey of two or three days or, as the Eskimo would say, two or three igloos. Each night, instead of pitching a tent as we would in the South, the Eskimo builds an igloo to house himself and the white man. The dogs burrow deeply into the snow. Once at their destination, the post takes on the air of a party, for few new faces are ever seen. The guests remain for several days to swap yarns and to hear such news as the northern grapevine can produce. Finally, they prepare to start back, and another messenger proceeds onward to the next post with the mail.

The Eskimos are a people with a summer and a winter home. In summer they live in tents. In winter they move to igloos. Because they depend largely on the sea for their supply of food, they rarely wander more than thirty to forty miles inland. For heat and light during the long winter they use the oil which they obtain from seals, walrus, whales, and bears. As a matter of fact, their food supply provides them with clothing and material for tents as well.

As extensive cooking in an igloo would not be practical, the Eskimos have solved the problem by eating their meat and fish raw. This is their chief food supply. They consume enormous quantities, as much as forty pounds a day for a family. To obtain such vast supplies they must hunt over a wide area and the fewer the inhabitants the better are their chances of survival. Tea seems to be the chief supplement to the meat diet. Eskimos will do almost anything for a few ounces of tea. It is the first thing they ask for when they see a white man. All ages drink it, strong, without milk or sugar—and they eat the tea leaves last of all.

Often their hunting takes them on a journey of several days from home. It may be that a herd of cariboo has been reported not far away. Or perhaps it is the walrus season, in which case they go by launch into the midst of mountainous, floating ice fields. Eskimos are equally skillful with gun or harpoon. They know that if they fail the first time, there is seldom a second chance, for at first scent of danger their prey vanishes.

When they come upon a good hunting area they kill as quickly and as widely as possible. Their booty is left where it falls in order to pursue the fleeing game. Later they will return to remove the hides, cut up the carcasses, and sort the meat, eating great quantities all the while. The less desirable portions are thrown to the dogs; the hides and certain choice cuts are put aside to be taken home; the rest goes to make up their evening feast, when they will gorge themselves until they fall over in a stupor. If the hunting has been especially successful, whole carcasses are buried under a pile of rocks to be left for other hunters who may pass that way.

What do the white men do with their time in the lonely, Arctic Hudson's Bay posts? There are long hours for reading, hunting, and talking, but there is plenty of work to be done too. Throughout the winter they pit their wits against Nature in an effort to stay alive. Their cabins become smaller and smaller as they close off room by room, and draw near the stove, to live and to sleep. August finds them preparing for the time when they may be unable to venture out of doors,—sorting their provisions, bringing together their foodstuffs, and arranging their fuel supply. To make their houses warmer, snow is piled heavily around the outside, with only the windows left clear.

By November the animals have grown fine, silky coats and the Eskimos and Indians are off trapping. When they return with a load of furs, the white man must have them cleaned, softened, cured, and baled, for next year's boat.

Money never passes in trading with the Eskimos. The measure of value is the "beaver skin." A load of furs is valued at so many beaver skins. The Eskimo may either take it out in store goods, or it may be applied to his credit. Frequently he owes a debt for the goods required for his hunting expedition. Contact with the outside world has changed his habits considerably. We have already noticed his devotion to tea and firearms. Plaid shawls, mirrors, toys, lard, and white men's clothes have an endless fascination for him. While occasionally from his tent issue sounds peculiar only to a phonograph, a typewriter, or a sewing machine!

At Cooking Lake, just outside Edmonton, the sun is shining brightly, and it is twenty degrees below zero. Six or seven planes, resting on their wide, wooden skis, are being warmed up. Mechanics are busy with last-minute checkups. A few passengers bundled in raccoon coats, leather trousers, and high Eskimo boots, stamp about. The freight and mail are loaded; the final weather report read; and the plane for the North is ready to start its eleven-hundred-mile trip to Port Radium. The few passengers climb in, to find places on top of crates and cases, for the plane carries no seats. It is used to bring supplies to the mining camps far in the north. It has carried important machinery, but today its load is largely fresh fruits and vegetables. The passengers settle themselves, and the plane moves off. Below, the earth is smooth and glistening white, broken only by the tracks of a little branch railway that runs as far as Waterways-McMurray. The cultivated farms vanish, to be followed by forests of pine and spruce. Frozen rivers and lakes seem to be everywhere. The skis are lowered and the plane lands with a sweep on the ice-covered Athabaska River. Under the shelter of the high walls along the riverbank, ice-bound steamers sleep out the winter. A growing pile of empty oil drums testifies to the traffic in this lonely country at the crossroads of the North. From here, planes will scatter in all directions. Some will go easterly to the gold mines of Lake Athabaska, some northwest following the fur-trading posts on the Mackenzie River, and others, like ourselves, due north to the gold and radium mines on Great Slave and Great Bear Lakes.

Port Radium, a town of several hundred people, is perched on the side of a cliff at the water's edge—a huddle of buildings covered with tarpaper or corrugated tin, built on several levels connected with each other by stairways up the side of the rock. Besides the mine itself, there are bunkhouses, a cookhouse, a recreation hall, a small hospital, and a radio station. It is not a prepossessing-looking place, but it is a fairly typical mining town.

In 1930, Port Radium was a vision in the eyes of a few men. Gilbert Labine had been a successful explorer and prospector for many years. His search for precious minerals took him into the Northwest Territories. People laughed at him. The idea of mining in the Arctic Circle seemed preposterous. He persevered however, and on the shores of Great Bear Lake he found a cliff containing many metals. Running through it were several veins of the highest quality pitchblende—that fabulous mineral from which Madame Curie extracted radium.

He tried to raise money to finance a mine. A gram of radium sold for $75,000. Belgium, with thirty grams a year, was the chief producer of this magic substance. Only thirty-five grams were produced by the entire world, and here was pitchblende in quantity, waiting to be mined. Canadians were skeptical. The risks were too great. How could machinery be taken up there? It required many hundred tons of pitchblende to secure one gram of radium. How could the pitchblende be brought out? Who would work so far north? The place was over a thousand miles from civilization, how could a community be fed?

Once again, Labine persisted and succeeded. His answer to much of the problem was the airplane. Tons of pitchblende were flown out to Edmonton, and machinery, provisions, experts, and workmen were flown in. The Belgians lowered the price of radium to $25,000 a gram. Still the company was able to produce, in spite of terrific transportation costs. Once well established Labine resorted to water transportation. The Mackenzie River had long been a summer highway for freight boats. Great Bear Lake could be used, and with a few portages, it was possible to get the large sacks of pitchblende to the railroad at Waterways-McMurray. Staple foods could be brought north by boat in summer, to be supplemented by regular air service for fresh eggs, fruits, and vegetables. Even with these economies, transportation costs run into big figures—slightly less than half a million dollars a year. Oil for the Diesel engines is transported from Norman Wells at a cost of about $110 a ton. Air express from Edmonton runs about seventy cents a pound, and a round-trip passenger ticket by air, from the same place, costs $350.

Most of the miners are young. They have come from the farm, the factory, and the classroom. Some will make mining their life work; others use it as a quick means of getting money to put them through college, or to buy a business. They are English, Scots, French, Finns, Slavs, Scandinavians—a miniature U.N.O.

Half of the men work days, and the remainder, nights. They dress for work in oilskins, with heavy rubber boots, a helmet that carries a lamp, and strong leather gloves. They make their way down the shaft, maybe a thousand or twelve hundred feet, and on through passages under the lake to the seam on which they are working. It is cold and damp. The water is trickling down the sides of the rock, and the temperature is just below freezing. They find their location and start to work in groups of two on a lot of loose rubble blasted by the men on the previous shift. One man operates the machinery that scoops up the rock and deposits it in a little car. The other guides the empty cars to be filled, and sends the loaded ones on their way. Toward the end of the day, power drills bore holes in the rocky walls. They are stuffed with explosives, and the fuses are lighted at the end of the shift.

When the men come up from the mine they shed their oilskins. These are put in a room to be dried and made ready for another shift. The men go into cubicles equipped with sun lamps, otherwise they could not continue to work in that land of perpetual twilight and biting frost. Then they are ready for a big meal of fresh meat and vegetables, pies and fruits. Maybe it is movie night, or perhaps they will play billiards, or plan for their return to the outside world. If they have been working for a couple of years they should have saved about $5,000.

The Eldorado Gold Mines, Ltd., for that is the name under which the company was organized, worked very successfully through the thirties. With the fall of France in 1940, the radium market dwindled. The mine closed, the pumps stopped, and the waters of Great Bear Lake flooded in. For nearly two years Radium City was a ghost town, occupied by only two men. Then the government took over the mine and reopened it, to operate under a shroud of secrecy. This time radium was not the goal,

Parliament Buildings and Peace Tower, Ottawa

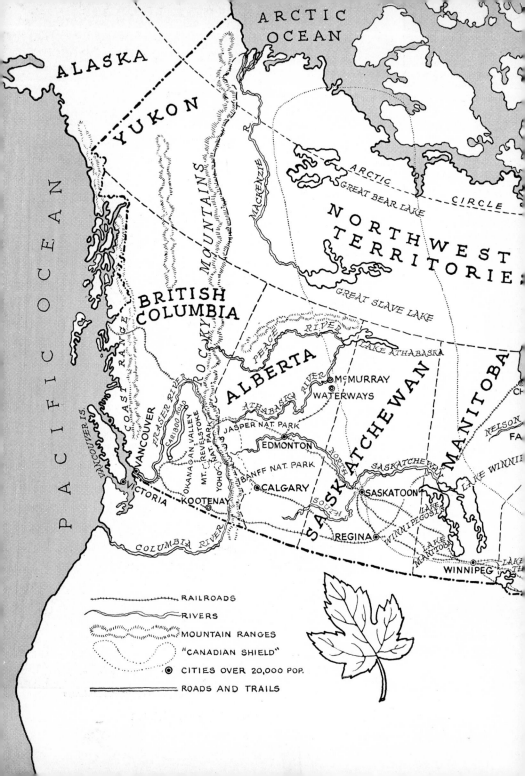

CHALEUR BAY GULF OF ST. LAWRENCE

NEW BRUNSWICK

MAINE

RESTIGOUCHE R.

ST. JOHN R.

NORTHUMBERLAND STRAIT

PRINCE EDWARD ISLAND

SUMMERSIDE

CAP ROUGE
CHETICAMP

CAPE BRETON ISLAND

CHARLOTTETOWN

BADDECK

CABOT TRAIL

SYDNEY

MONCTON

ST. JOHN

PICTOU

STRAIT OF CANSO

LOUISBURG

BRAS D'OR LAKES

BAY OF FUNDY

GRAND PRE

ST. CROIX RIVER

NOVA SCOTIA

ANNAPOLIS ROYAL

HALIFAX

LUNENBURG

YARMOUTH

ATLANTIC OCEAN

HUDSON BAY

LABRADOR

OCEAN

QUEBEC

ONTARIO

NEWFOUNDLAND

LAURENTIANS

SHIPSHAW R.

SAGUENAY RIVER

ST. LAWRENCE R.

GASPÉ

GASPE ROAD

CHALEUR BAY

CAP ROUGE
CHETICAMP

CAPE BRETON ISLAND

SYDNEY

LOUISBURG

ARVIDA

MURRAY BAY

N.B.

P.E.I.

TIMMINS

KIRKLAND LAKE

ROUYN

OTTAWA

QUEBEC

MONCTON

PICTOU

ST. JOHN

GRAND PRÉ

THETFORD

HALIFAX

LUNENBURG

ANNAPOLIS ROYAL

RIOR

SAULT Ste. MARIE

COBALT

SUDBURY

NORTH BAY

LAKE NIPISSING

OTTAWA R.

MONTREAL

OTTAWA

KINGSTON

BAY of FUNDY

YARMOUTH

NOVA SCOTIA

RIOR

MICHIGAN

HURON

GEORGIAN BAY

MUSKOKA LAKES

ONTARIO

TORONTO

ERIE

ATLANTIC

Percé

Chateau Frontenac and the Citadel, Quebec

St. Henri de Taillon, Quebec

A French Bake Oven, Quebec

Halifax

Evangeline Memorial Church, Grande Pré

Logging in British Columbia

Logger Handling Boom Logs, British Columbia

Canadian Pacific Railway Co.

Reversing Falls, Saint John, New Brunswick

Place d'Armes, Montreal

Excavating the Canal at Shipshaw, Saguenay

Saulte Ste. Marie Canal

The Calgary Stampede

Royal Canadian Mounted Police at Jasper Park

Jasper National Park

Canadian Pacific Railway Co.

Combines at Work, Western Canada

Salmon Running Upstream, British Columbia

Provincial Government Building, Victoria, B.C.

Hudson's Bay Company Post, Manitoba

Hudson's Bay Company Post, Baker Lake

A Trading Post off the Eastern Arctic

Squaw and Child, Alberta Foothills

Eskimo Kayak Race, Hudson Strait

Mount Robson and a Canadian Railway Train

Canadian National Railways

Mond Nickel Mine, Coniston, Ontario

Spinning in Quebec

Ste. Anne de Beaupré, Quebec

Canadian Air Highway to Russia and the East

Cabot Trail

Looking North on Bay St., Toronto

Fishing Fleet at Lunenberg, Nova Scotia

"The Bore," Moncton, New Brunswick

but uranium for the atom bomb!

When Labine proved it could be done, the rush started. Representatives of other large mining companies were soon busy in the vicinity. The costs of transportation, the difficulty of shelter and food, makes it virtually impossible for the independent prospector to work so far from supplies. Only during the two months of summer is it possible to explore the territory. A tent is inadequate protection for winter, lumber not available, and food supplies nonexistent.

The rush to Great Bear Lake led many to explore the mineral possibilities of Great Slave Lake to the south. Gold was once again the irresistible magnet. Claims were staked and diamond drills disclosed startling veins of gold. One little company owning a claim sold out for half a million in cash and a forty per cent interest in the business. Canada was in the throes of another gold rush. This time the town of Yellowknife was in the headlines. Although only a small portion of the area has been prospected, over one hundred and thirty companies have been organized to work in the vicinity of Yellowknife. Prospectors, geologists, and mining engineers are still working their way into remote districts of the North.

Between the two extremes of civilization, the Eskimo on the one hand, and the miner on the other, is a third group, made up of Indians, half-breeds, and an occasional white man who has drifted into the North and likes it so well that he cannot leave. Most of these people are trappers. Some of them live in the North only during the winter season and return to their families for the summer. Others, without home ties, prefer to remain in their lonely cabins all the year round. One trip to civilization (the Hudson's Bay post), is sufficient to dispose of their year's harvest of furs and to obtain supplies for the coming winter. A few days stop to swap yarns and adventures with each other and the trappers are eager to return home to their lonely log cabins.

CHAPTER VIII

◊◊ *The Founding of French Canada* ◊◊

FRANCE, when she undertook to create an empire beyond the seas, was the foremost nation of Europe in population and armed might, in art and education, in manners and fashion. England, although she had recently defeated the Spanish Armada, was considerably less powerful. Each of these countries established its first permanent settlement in the New World within a year of the other. Jamestown was founded in 1607, and Quebec the following year. Within sixty years, England already had a number of flourishing colonies along the Atlantic seaboard and was about to complete the chain by capturing New York from the Dutch, while France could point only to Quebec, Three Rivers, Montreal, and Acadia, whose settlers together comprised but a small fraction of the English population to the south and which could claim to be little more than trading posts.

For years the few hardy Frenchmen who followed Champlain to Quebec were forced to be content with help both uncertain and insufficient. France's kings and ministers seemingly failed to realize the possibilities which the new continent possessed. The colony, remote and uninviting at best, not only failed to produce the hoped-for wealth, but, instead, was a constant financial drain on the mother country.

Jacques Cartier, the first Frenchman to make his way to the St. Lawrence, sailed up the river in 1534, visited the Indian settlement of Stadacona, and returned to France. On two later occasions he came back, and, together with his shipmates, wintered on the present site of Quebec, then an Indian settlement. Sixty years passed.

From a new generation came Samuel de Champlain in 1603. As geographer of the Court of France, he made several voyages, charting the St. Lawrence, the coast of Nova Scotia, and northern New England. In 1604 he was with the founders of Port Royal, Nova Scotia, then called Acadia. In 1608, under his leadership, the first permanent French settlement was made, on the site of Cartier's previous attempt, Quebec. The little colony struggled along in spite of overwhelming odds. Its existence was due to Champlain's untiring efforts to win and keep the support of the neighboring Indians, and to gain what aid he could from such influential, French families as he might persuade to push the cause of the colony at Court.

In 1629 Champlain was forced to surrender Quebec to the English, and to be carried away as a prisoner of war. The government of France lost interest and more or less left the people to the mercy of the Iroquois, whose raids became increasingly frequent and intense.

Years passed. Louis XIV sat on the throne. His chief minister, Colbert, recognized the possibilities possessed by the little colonies in New France and determined to make them a source of strength to the mother country. He converted the king to his point of view. The colonies were brought directly under the control of the King, to be ruled by a Sovereign Council, appointed by him and responsible to him. France had no intention of permitting popular government. But then, it would have been strange if she had, for her citizens at home enjoyed no such privileges. Actually, the plan of government put into effect corresponded closely to that in force in the provinces of France. Almost every detail of life was carefully regulated. The council, among other things, controlled trade, fixed prices, determined the amount of profits, regulated agriculture and industry, and tried and punished lawbreakers.

Three members of the council, the governor, the bishop, and the intendant, were chief in command. The governor was the leading public and military figure, responsible for defense and for negotiations with the Indian tribes. The bishop was charged with the religious life of the colony, its education, and its hospitals. The intendant administered justice and promoted the public welfare through commerce and industry. The duties of these officials overlapped. For instance, in the ever-present Indian question, who was to have the deciding voice? The bishop, the intendant, and the governor each were concerned with these tribes from a different standpoint. This overlapping of authority was intentional. The theory behind the idea was that each official, by watching the others, would prevent either of them from exerting too much power, or, failing that, would complain to the home government.

The new officials when they arrived in Quebec were accompanied by the first body of regular soldiers to be sent from France. These men, together with many of the settlers, thirteen hundred strong and wise in the ways of the Indian, marched into the Lake Champlain region, the home of the Iroquois. The Iroquois fled before the advancing soldiers, completely terrified at so great a show of strength. The following year they sent messengers to Quebec to sue for peace, and a brighter day dawned for the colonies along the St. Lawrence.

One of the most glorious chapters in the history of New France tells of the men and women who were inspired to found churches, schools, hospitals, and Indian missions. Although many religious orders contributed to this cause, the hardships, disappointments, and martyrdom suffered by the Jesuits are without parallel. Their task was disheartening beyond belief. Frequently the Indian did not want their Christian ministrations. His superstitions, his belief in magic, his ceremonials and feasts were the result of old tradition. In warfare he was brutal, sometimes going to the extreme of cannibalism. Yet through it all the lonely missionary persisted on his way. He endured long journeys with scanty food, heavy labor, and disheartenment, in order that he might learn to understand the Indian and to win him for Christ.

Every missionary, trained to careful observation, was required to give an account of his work, of his travels, and of his life with the Indians. Each year these reports, known as the *Jesuit Relations*, were published in France where they aroused tremendous interest, and were a source of inspiration to other pious people who, in turn, established convents, hospitals, and seminaries in the New World. Collected into seventy-three volumes, the *Jesuit Relations* are one of the most valuable sources of information on the French colonies.

Montreal owes its origin, in 1642, to religious zeal. A group of soldiers, priests, and nuns ventured far into the wilderness, in defiance of advice and caution, at a time when the Iroquois menaced even Quebec. Nothing but the dauntless courage of religious fervor would have prompted such a hazardous undertaking.

François Xavier de Laval-Montmorency, Jean Talon, and Comte de Frontenac stand out as the great figures of early Canadian history. Laval came to Quebec in 1659 as the Vicar Apostolic or chief spiritual advisor of the colony. His influence on its destiny and morals was to be decisive. Laval was a highly admirable figure, a born leader who could not endure to yield or to lag behind, a man of unswerving determination, scholarly, and physically rugged. He aimed to make the Church the most powerful influence in the life of the colony. Laval's great influence and claim to fame rests on his skill in organizing the clergy, in encouraging hospitals, and in founding two seminaries. He fought a losing battle—the hottest and most famous cause of dispute between himself and his fellow officials—over the sale of brandy to the Indians. In this quarrel Laval was opposed by Talon, and later by Frontenac. Each official, jealously guarding that which he considered himself bound to defend, battled over this ever-annoying problem. The Church firmly opposed the use of brandy in the fur trade. The Indian was degraded by it, and the Christian religion mocked. To the Intendant—and to the businessman—

who had the commercial welfare of the colony at heart, the problem assumed a different aspect. They argued that if the French did not sell brandy to the Indian, the English would ply him with rum, and thus not only would France suffer, but the Indian also, by being subjected to Protestant heresy. It should be understood that the leaders of France were devout in their feeling for and performance of religious obligations. It was only when the Church invaded fields not strictly religious that friction resulted.

Talon, the first and greatest Intendant, has been called "the colonial Colbert." He arrived to find Quebec a sickly colony. He worked to increase her population, to improve her agriculture, to create industry and mining, and to augment trade. His efforts, on the whole, were successful. At his own expense he ordered a ship to be built in order to demonstrate that shipbuilding was possible. He had horses and sheep brought over from France. He mingled experienced pioneers with newcomers, started a model farm, introduced the growing of hemp, prospected for minerals, encouraged weaving, built a tannery, and a score of other innovations. Within a few years of his arrival he was able to report, "I am now clothed from foot to head with homemade articles." When he discovered that the regiment brought over to quell the Indians was willing to be discharged and remain in the country, he encouraged them to settle along the Richelieu, the gateway through which the Iroquois were wont to attack.

He recognized that no colony could thrive without a growing population. He enlisted Colbert's support and for several years colonists arrived in large numbers. Wives, especially, were needed, for there were many more men than women in the colony. Shiploads of marriageable young women, carefully selected in France, were sent out, and few remained unchosen at the end of a fortnight. In addition, Talon promoted marriage indirectly by penalizing bachelors—they were not permitted to hunt or fish, or to trade with the Indians. When he left Quebec in 1672, he could claim to have more than doubled its population. His demand for colonists had been so incessant as to lead Colbert to declare that he would not "unpeople France for the purpose of peopling Canada." However, had the government of France only recognized it, a small fraction of the men so carelessly lost on European battlefields—and the Protestants forbidden to emigrate—would have made Canada a really thriving country. For a brief period of some six or seven years, due chiefly to the enthusiasm of Talon, emigration flourished. Had this growth continued, there would have been over half a million inhabitants by 1750, sufficient to repel the English conquest. Unfortunately Talon's vision was not shared by others, and no further extensive colonization was carried on. This leaves us with an interesting result—the population of French Canada today is to a large degree descended from the colonists brought over by Talon in the third quarter of the seventeenth century.

The third great leader, Frontenac, the Iron Governor, was a man of great physical endurance, strong will, shrewd judgment, and boundless courage. Frontenac believed in action. Within a few months of his arrival he called a meeting of the Indians at Lake Ontario, met them with an impressive display of pageantry, received the chieftains in state, listened gravely to their orations, and in return made an impressive address in the Indian manner. All this time, under their astonished eyes, at forced speed, French workmen were erecting a fort. Needless to say, this exhibition had its effect, and while Frontenac remained as governor, no Indian outrages disturbed the progress of the colony. Unfortunately his highhandedness brought about unpleasantness with Laval and the Intendant, and he was recalled in 1682. His incompetent successors, unable to handle the Indians and having undone all that Frontenac had accomplished, once more put the colony in danger of attack. War between England and France broke out, and the Iroquois, allies of the British, were on the warpath again. Frontenac, hurriedly reinstated, devoted himself to planning and directing the necessary military operations. Both English and French colonists suffered in the savage raids. An English fleet even appeared before the citadel of Quebec to demand surrender. However, with Frontenac in command, the bombardment which followed proved a waste of ammunition, and the fleet retired.

Frontenac's vision gave France the right to claim the vast western territories. He was impressed with the stragetic importance of exploring the West, and with the necessity of guarding the routes over which the fur trade travelled. (Joliet, Marquette, and La Salle all explored under his encouragement and guidance.) He was responsible for the building of the forts on Lakes Ontario, Michigan, and in the Illinois area. His policy, a thorn in the side of England, was definitely in the interests of France.

The great majority of settlers were farmers, tilling the soil in a rather primitive fashion, and supporting themselves as best they could by their own labors. Frontier life, wherever it may be, follows a more or less similar pattern. The seigniorial system of land ownership had been transferred from France just as the freehold system was transferred from England to New England. The habitants in Canada were protected from exploitation by a written contract, and were free from many of the restrictions widely prevalent in France. Social barriers were practically nonexistent. The seigneur's home was little better than theirs, and frequently he could be seen working in the fields also. Families were large and many hands were needed.

Everybody wanted to live beside the water, and, while available land remained, they did so, with the result that both sides of the St. Lawrence and the smaller rivers flowing into it, resembled long highways bordered on each side by a continuous row of little white cottages. The settlers held their land in long, narrow strips, but cultivated only that nearest the water, enough to supply their own needs, with a small margin for sale. The habitants were better fed and better clothed than the people of France. Beaver, a luxury in Paris, was a common sight in Quebec. The houses were built of either logs or stone, and each spring a fresh coat of white-wash was applied. The living quarters on the first floor were supplemented by a row of beds in the garret above, to accommodate the large family. Horses became plentiful and each habitant possessed at least one. Oxen were used for farm work and the horse, rather well cared for, was reserved largely for pleasure. Feudalism in Canada was a very different thing from that practiced in the Old World. With a scarcity of available tenants, the habitant could and did command terms undreamed of in France.

The long winter months were filled with gaiety. The chores soon over, there was little to do but have a good time. Cards, dancing, story telling, singing, visiting—an almost endless round of festivity was the order of the day. Many people have since called these habitants ignorant, because few of them could read, but education was not an important part of pioneering life, either there or anywhere. The French knew and practiced one important thing—how to enjoy life.

Although the settlers were largely farmers, the lure of the forest proved irresistible to many men. Few families there were that did not have at least one member who had become a *coureur de bois*. It was a lawless, dangerous and fascinating life, in the woods, trapping, trading, and sometimes living with the Indians. The Church frowned on it and tried to prevent it. The government in France passed decrees providing severe penalities, fines, confiscation, even death, but it was futile. One governor wrote, "I cannot tell you how attractive this life is to all our youth. It consists in doing nothing, caring nothing, following every inclination, and getting out of the way of all restraint." Though this occupation drained New France of a much needed population, without these *coureurs de bois*, who knew the wilds, the fur trade could never have been continued successfully. Who knows, had there not been the lure of the fur trade to distract many from settling down to steady, honest, hard, farm work, the entire history of the country might have taken a different course.

As we know, the English were not idle during the period that saw France seeking to establish herself along the St. Lawrence River. From the founding of Jamestown in 1607, English colonies had multiplied along the Atlantic coast.

In 1670, stirred by the wealth to be gained from the fur trade, the Hudson's Bay Company was created. After 1670, North America was cut up into several areas. The Hudson's Bay Company and the American colonies were both English; New France, or Canada and Acadia were both French; Mexico and the Gulf of Mexico area belonged to Spain. The French saw themselves with English to the north and south. Their more or less undisputed possession of the valuable fur trade was now being challenged by the Hudson's Bay Company. Frontenac was aware of this danger and, as we have already noted, had constructed a chain of forts from Lake Ontario into the Illinois area, in order to break through the threatened encirclement, and to make it possible to obtain furs from the Indians in the heart of their own country. Eventually the French held a thin line of settlements stretching from the St. Lawrence via the Great Lakes and the Mississippi to the Gulf of Mexico.

War broke out on the continent of Europe between England and France, in 1689. From that time onward until 1763, with brief truces intervening, North America was a battlefield for opposing forces.

When Quebec was founded, France was the foremost nation in Europe. In the intervening years, England had grown more wealthy and more powerful. Her commerce expanded, her navy grew stronger, and her colonies more prosperous. In spite of the fact that each country had begun its colonizing activities at about the same time, there were eight times as many English as French in North America by 1713, and thirty times as many by 1750. The English were settlers. They came in large numbers. They were expanding westward, and would eventually destroy the fur trade on which the French economy was built. France was not willing, naturally enough, to acknowledge that the English were more successful than she, nor was she willing to relinquish her position in North America. Obviously, fur trading and farming could not exist side by side. One country or the other must prevail. Both had sought to please the Indians, the French more successfully than the English. The Frenchman's charm of manner, his adaptability to life in the woods, the zeal of his missionaries, and the religious system, appealing as it did to the imagination of the Indian, all combined to give him greater influence with the native tribes. The Englishman, on the other hand, be he in the settlement or roaming the forests, lacked these qualities. His one advantage over his rival was an ability to pay higher prices for furs, and to sell to the Indian more cheaply. This last quality won over the Iroquois. These tribes, by reason of their strategic location between the French and English settlements, played one nation off against the other, resulting in much bloodshed.

Throughout the struggle which lasted about seventy years, France slowly lost ground. In 1713, she ceded Acadia to England for the last time, but she still retained all her other holdings. The French and Indian War finally brought the duel to a close. By the Treaty of Paris in 1763, France renounced all claim to North America, and retained only two small islands off the coast of Newfoundland, St. Pierre and Miquelon, for the drying of fish.

Why did France lose her empire in North America? There are many answers to this question. For one thing the manpower in New France was hopelessly outnumbered by that of the English colonies. For many years, while new settlements were springing up along the Atlantic seaboard, the French had been dissipating their energies in the hopeless task of trying to find a northwest passage to Asia. It was not by accident that the French chose the St. Lawrence as a likely location for a settlement. What other opening along the Atlantic coast appeared so promising? From that they turned to the fur trade which provided immediate wealth for an extravagant court.

The French colonists were given no chance to think for themselves. Every colonial problem, no matter how trivial, was regulated in France by men who had no idea of the needs of the settlers. The intentional overlapping of duties, which the government of France fostered, proved to be a disaster when the siege of Quebec was at stake. The story of Montcalm's gallant but ineffectual defense of the colony in the face of overwhelming British superiority under Wolfe, is an excellent example of the orders and counterorders which his rivalry brought about. In spite of the efficient espionage system which the overlapping of authority was intended to produce, fraud and graft were, in later years, practiced on a grand scale in both Quebec and in Louisburg, the fortress which France built on Cape Breton Island to guard the entrance to the St. Lawrence. Forts were constructed of inferior materials, at very slow speed, in order to spin out the job and to make more money.

The English colonists could put up an impressive struggle by their own efforts. New France was dependent upon the mother country for all her military supplies. When the British intercepted the ships bound for New France, as they did on every opportunity, the results were disastrous. Now the British Navy had been steadily growing since 1588, that momentous date that marks the defeat of the Spanish Armada. The Atlantic, to France a barrier, was now to England a highway. In time of war French merchant ships, and even the navy, were at the mercy of Britain. The British Navy proved to be an obstacle which France could not vanquish. In the final analysis, the nation destined to win the duel was the one that could command the seas.

CHAPTER IX

⋄⋄ *Early Days in British North America* ⋄⋄

THE WORD "CANADA," until 1867, referred exclusively to that part of British North America now known as the provinces of Quebec and Ontario. When Britain acquired the land from France in 1763, settlements were confined to the shores of the St. Lawrence and the small tributary rivers flowing into it. In 1713, France had ceded her eastern colony, Acadia, to Britain, who renamed it Nova Scotia. Halifax had been founded as a garrison town and station for the North Atlantic Fleet. In the following years many settlers from the American colonies arrived in Nova Scotia. These people had no intention of giving up their English privileges, and they were determined to remake Nova Scotia according to their own plan. This they proceeded to do, even though it meant driving the Acadians from their farms, and transporting them to the American colonies.

When Britain fell heir to Quebec, she acquired a sizeable number of people, alien in language, religion, customs, and laws. The government fully intended to Anglicize the French Canadians, but the British governor in charge recognized the folly and futility of such a plan and evaded it. In the years immediately following the capitulation of Quebec and Montreal, there had arrived a motley assortment of British Protestants, whom the governor called the "grab-alls" and "Americanized camp-following traders." These people were desirous of obtaining wealth in the newly acquired colony. They were to be the cause of much dissatisfaction and strife. Having been accustomed to representative government, they demanded it in Quebec. The fact that the French Canadians were unaccustomed to it made little difference to them. In fact, their plan would have included in the government only such as could comply with the anti-Roman Catholic laws then in force in England. Their repeated demands for representative government and their general unscrupulousness in dealing with the French served to waken the government in Britain to the need of an act to safeguard the rights of the latter—thus the Quebec Act of 1774, frequently called the Magna Carta of the French Canadian race.

Justice demanded that the conflicting system of laws in force should be settled. The French unaccustomed to British law, continued to regulate their lives by their own code. In England, Roman Catholics were denied the right to vote or to hold public office, but to do so in Canada would be equivalent to committing them to government without any representation. Some form of legislative government must be provided. The growing dissatisfaction in the thirteen colonies demanded the conciliation of the French Canadian population.

By the Quebec Act, French Canadians were guaranteed the "free exercise of the Religion of the Church of Rome," and Roman Catholics could hold public office. Old French law was retained for all civil cases, while English law was to prevail in criminal cases. The making of laws was entrusted to a governor and a council, all to be royally appointed. The boundaries of the Province of Quebec were defined to extend from Labrador on the east to the Mississippi on the west, and to the Ohio River on the south, and the seigniorial system was left undisturbed.

By defining the position of the Church, and the land ownership rights of the seigneurs, the British won the allegiance of clerical leaders and of the so-called aristocracy—a result of no mean importance in view of the rising temper of the American colonists. Any Anglicizing which had been accomplished was checked. The antiquated and intricate French law was perpetuated—later to prove a real obstacle to the commercial progress of the province. While the Quebec Act laid the groundwork for an alliance between Church and State, which was to prove influential in many future crises, the English minority were more disgruntled than ever. They failed to get representative government and they were forced to accept Roman Catholics in government posts.

The Act caused tremendous resentment in the American colonies. The Puritans of New England were highly incensed by the virtual establishment of the Roman Catholic religion in Quebec, while the boundary settlement was outrageous. It took away their opportunity for westward expansion north of the Ohio River. Coming as it did, hard on the heels of the repressive measures instituted in retaliation for the Boston Tea Party, the colonists refused to believe that its chief principles had been agreed upon before news of that event arrived in England.

The problem of governing an alien people was difficult, and the British had no previous experience to guide them. One man recognized the solution and urged it in repeated reports to the government. That man was Sir Guy Carleton, later Baron Dorchester, who became governor of Quebec in 1766. His main point was that Canada would retain its French characteristics for the simple reason that it would never attract sufficient English-speaking people to alter the balance of population. He urged that Britain should provide a government made up of the local leaders, otherwise the loyalty of the French Canadians would remain with France, and Britain would be faced with future trouble.

There is still a wide difference of opinion as to whether the Quebec Act was a sound plan. It seemed to provide a solution at the time, for, as we shall see, the great majority remained loyal to Britain despite all efforts to gain their support for the American Revolution.

The effect of the Revolution was felt in Canada almost immediately. In the thirteen colonies the view was widely held that Quebec, "the 14th state," as it was frequently called, whose population was composed of a conquered people, would welcome deliverance at the hands of the American patriots. Consequently, two armies were dispatched northward in 1775, one to take Montreal, and the other to capture Quebec. In addition, three Americans, one of whom was Benjamin Franklin, were appointed by the Continental Congress to persuade Canada to join the war. Both plans failed. The armies were defeated and the commissioners with their printing press made little impression on the habitant, who was largely illiterate. The Quebec Act, by guaranteeing French customs and the Roman Catholic religion, had won the support of the clergy and of the seignieurs.

The American Revolution changed the whole course of Canadian history. The Loyalists in the United States, or, as they are known to Americans, the Tories, migrated to Canada in increasing numbers. Many of them had disapproved of the British system of taxation, but they opposed independence as the solution. Others, who supported Britain as the likely winner of the contest, found that their judgment had been wrong. These people were largely English and many of them were passionately devoted to the Crown. Their coming complicated the problem of government, and hastened the introduction of the free institutions to which they had always been accustomed. Thus the American Revolution made Canada a nation composed of two groups, alien to each other in language, race, customs, and religion.

As Carleton had predicted, few English-speaking people settled along the St. Lawrence River. A small number of the Loyalists, fleeing from the American Revolution, remained there, but the great majority moved into the interior and settled west of the Ottawa River, along the northern shore of Lake Ontario.

The arrival of so many English settlers in Canada necessitated revision of the plan of government. The Quebec Act was no longer useful. It had been drawn up to provide for the French. The English demanded representative government. They had been accustomed to it, and they were justified in their demand. Obviously the French could not be denied what the English were to be granted.

The British government finally decided to divide British North

America into two provinces, Upper Canada to be composed of English people, and Lower Canada of French. They introduced the form of colonial government so hated by the American colonists—that of a governor, an elective assembly, and a council appointed by the governor for life. This time there was a difference, however. Britain had learned a lesson from the American Revolution and she was determined to avoid a repetition of that unfortunate affair. She guaranteed the position of the Roman Catholic Church in Lower Canada; and in Upper Canada, the maintenance and support of the Protestant Church.

Once again there is a wide difference of opinion as to whether the decision to separate the French from the English was a wise one. Certainly the English minority in Lower Canada were far from satisfied. They used all the influence they could muster to gain an advantage over the French, a situation which certainly did not contribute to good feeling. The elective assembly was composed largely of French Canadians with a sprinkling of Englishmen, who held office by courtesy of the French vote. The council, appointed by the governor who represented the Crown and was himself an Englishman, was composed largely of his fellow countrymen. No bill could become law until it had received the consent of both legislative bodies and the approval of the governor. Here we have the makings of a racial struggle, for the English wielded power out of all proportion to their numbers.

In Upper Canada the struggle was not to be racial but rather one between two factions, those who held the reins of government and those who wished to have a voice in the control of their own affairs. Now government appointments were for life and in the event of a vacancy, office holders made sure that it was filled by one of their own group.

Although the American colonies had obtained their independence, peace did not bring good will. The United States was angry because the British continued to hold the northwest posts; while Britain charged the United States with failure to live up to the provisions of the peace treaty which would have compensated the Loyalists. The boundaries outlined in the peace treaty of 1783 were inaccurate. For example, the St. Croix River on the east was to divide Maine from New Brunswick. No less than three rivers might have been the St. Croix. West of Lake Superior the line was to be drawn through little lakes and rivers to the Lake of the Woods, and from there *due west* to the source of the Mississippi River, whereas that river had its origin far to the south. In the West, the Indians were causing trouble, which the United States laid to British intrigue. The French Revolution eventually involved Britain and other European nations in war with the new republic. Pro-French sentiment in the United States proved difficult. Gênet, the French ambassador to the United States sent agents into Canada to enlist French support, and loose talk of a French invasion of Quebec, with Republican aid from the United States, caused alarm.

Many refugee French priests, exiled by the Revolution, arrived in Lower Canada, and as might well be expected, their sympathies were not with the republican government of France. From that time onward, the clergy directed their efforts toward keeping the province true to Old France.

As can be seen, Canada was automatically involved in this verbal struggle. Her geographical location now, as in later crises, was to have a profound influence on the policy which both the United States and Great Britain adopted toward each other and toward her.

Britain had been at war with France for a number of years, but with Napoleon's rise to power, the struggle had assumed life-and-death proportions. In an attempt to cripple one another, both Britain and France had imposed a blockade to prevent neutral ships from providing supplies to the other. Nations at war need many things. The United States was only too ready to supply those needs. Trouble arose with England because she had the navy necessary to make her blockade effective, while the French restrictions were largely confined to threats on paper.

In addition to confiscating goods destined for France, Britain claimed the right to search neutral ships at sea, and to seize deserters from her navy. Now many English seamen were deserting their ships. Conditions were bad in the British Navy and these sailors were attracted by the better opportunities for employment and the higher wages offered by prosperous United States shippers. In order to reman its ships, the Royal Navy searched American vessels and seized deserters—and occasionally American citizens, some of whom were actually citizens and others who held forged papers, a practice common enough at that time. In spite of growing protests from the United States, Britain felt obliged to continue the practice, in view of the desperate situation in which she found herself. Remember that without a navy she would have been at the mercy of Napoleon.

Feeling between the two countries mounted. The 1810 elections brought into Congress a number of young men who urged a vigorous policy in defense of American rights. The War Hawks, as they were called, were eager to further westward expansion in the United States. They sought to annex Canada. (John C. Calhoun urged that Canada could be conquered in four weeks.)

The War of 1812 brought an invasion of Canada—a three-pronged attack via Lake Champlain, Detroit, and Niagara. Canada faced a difficult problem of defense. Her population was little more than half a million, including many French Canadians and recent immigrants from the United States, the loyalty of the latter seriously open to question. In resources she was out-classed by the United States in the ratio of about fifteen to one. Despite these handicaps she made a remarkable showing. Both sides won victories and suffered reverses. The battles of Queenston Heights and Lundy's Lane aroused in Canadians a feeling of national pride comparable to that of Bunker Hill and Lexington of the Revolutionary War.

The American Fleet under Oliver Hazard Perry made a remark-

able showing on the Great Lakes, and United States forces captured York (now Toronto), the capital of Upper Canada, and
burned the parliament buildings—the presence of the Speaker's
wig hanging by his chair was considered evidence of the scalpings
to which Canada was reputed to be a party. In the Atlantic, the
United States Navy, insignificant as it was at that time, distinguished itself. It won several important duels, inflicted serious
loss on British trade, and kept a greatly superior naval force employed constantly. In the long run, however, the strength of the
British Navy was felt, and by 1814, a blockade of the Atlantic
coast was strangling American shipping. The British attacked
Washington, and burned the government buildings in retaliation
for the destruction in York the previous year.

In the judgment of historians of both countries, the war was a
serious blunder, unnecessary and avoidable. For Canada it had
important consequences. The peace treaty in 1815 provided for
the restoration of all occupied territory, the boundary still in
dispute to be settled by joint commission. Naval warfare on the
Great Lakes made evident the possibility of future rivalry. When
the United States therefore, proposed disarmament, Britain
agreed, and the Rush-Bagot Agreement was signed in 1817. This
put an end to any scramble for naval control, by providing for
disarmament on the Lakes. The forty-ninth parallel became the
boundary to the Rocky Mountains, and Americans were permitted
to share the coastal fishing privileges off Newfoundland, Labrador,
and the Magellan Islands.

Canada's heroic defense in the face of a much more powerful
invader served to develop a spirit of nationalism in the country.
The patriotism shown by French Canada was laudable, certainly
equal to that of British Upper Canada. One of the most brilliant
victories of the entire war, the Battle of Châteauguay, was won by
French Canadians, under their own commander, Salaberry. Also,
the war proved once more to the United States that Canada was
not willing to change flags.

CHAPTER X

⋙ *A Half Century of Growth* ⋘

THE WEST HAS ALWAYS played an important role in Canadian history. This is true because for over two hundred years the fur trade dominated to a large degree the life of the country. The story of exploration and development west of Ontario must be told in terms of the traders.

To go back to the seventeenth century, Henry Hudson, in search of the Northwest Passage, discovered the large bay in northern Canada which bears his name. It was a forbidding, ice-bound region, and lay neglected for many years. Strangely enough, Britain's knowledge of the wealth to be gained from this land came from two French traders, who, disappointed by the treatment of their own government, made their way to England. Thus the famous Hudson's Bay Company, destined to influence the course of Canadian history for nearly two hundred years, was born in 1670. Its membership was recruited from wealthy English families. They enjoyed great profits while seated at their own firesides, and left the labor to competent, reliable agents who went into the Northland, established trading posts, dealt with the Indians, and sent home shiploads of valuable pelts. Their charter gave them a monopoly of all the land draining into Hudson Bay. A glance at the map will show how tremendous was the area under their control. They built their chief post, York Factory, at the mouth of the Nelson River, and the Indians brought their furs to the company's posts. The fact that they did not pursue the Indians, but rather received them on home ground, will be of significance later.

As may well be imagined, the French in Montreal were not

willing to sit idly by while the British tapped the fur trade more nearly at its source. Raiding parties captured or destroyed the company's forts with little regard for the relations existing between Britain and France.

With the downfall of the French empire in America, New Englanders, Scots, and Englishmen hastened to Montreal, there to make a fortune in furs. (These were the men who caused so much trouble for the government in Quebec.) They organized the North West Company, affiliated themselves with French coureurs de bois, already adept at the game, and soon began to push aggressively westward. The Montreal traders realized that they were handicapped by the Hudson's Bay Company, which was located more nearly in the heart of the richest fur-bearing region. A thousand miles of travel via water and difficult portages considerably increased the expenses of the North West Company. To survive competition, they must go to the Indian, for he could not be expected to travel the extra distance when there existed a ready market near at hand. By purchasing the furs at their source, both the Indian and the North West Company profited. The latter, by being able to buy more cheaply, could absorb the extra cost of transportation, and many of the Indians were relieved of the chore of carrying their goods to the Hudson's Bay Company. Thus began a race which was to last for almost half a century.

The North West Company built their main outpost at Fort William on Lake Superior. They were aggressive. They went to the Indian. They used sound business tactics to promote their cause. Whereas the Hudson's Bay Company was operated by agents whose orders came from English owners, this new company, organized in Montreal was free from absentee control. Ambitious young men, if successful in the western outposts, might look forward to promotion, even to a directorship in the company. When we consider also that many of the traders and practically all the canoemen were French Canadians, born and bred to the wilds and to the shooting of rapids, it is only too apparent that this new company would provide keen competition for the Hudson's Bay Company.

It is to the North West Company that we owe the exploration of the West. They had to keep ahead of the Hudson's Bay Company or be ruined. The plains provided buffalo chiefly. It was to the north therefore that they must go in order to find the more valuable beaver pelts. The story of the opening of the Northwest is the story of the greatest of the fur-trading explorers. Alexander Mackenzie came to Canada from Scotland at the age of ten. At twenty-five he was in charge of trade for the North West Company in the far Northwest, at Lake Athabaska. He was eager to find out where the Athabaska and Peace rivers flowed. When his work for the season was over in 1789, four birch-bark canoes, containing eight European people, two of them women, and a number of Indians for guides, set out northward. On and on they went, into the land of the midnight sun, until they came to the shores of the Arctic Ocean. There Mackenzie ordered a post to be erected, on which he carved his name, the latitude, 69° 14′, and the number of persons accompanying him. He arrived back at his post after a voyage of 102 days, in which he had covered some three thousand miles by canoe, and had discovered one of the large rivers of the world, fittingly named in his honor—the Mackenzie River.

Three years later he was once more on his way, this time westward to find the source of the Peace River. In preparation for the trip he had constructed a birch-bark canoe, twenty-five feet in length, and capable of carrying a three-thousand-pound load. He ascended the Peace River, crossed the Great Divide, and reached the Pacific at the mouth of the Bella Coola River. There he inscribed, in red letters on a large rock, the memorable words: "Alexander Mackenzie, from Canada, by land, the twenty-second of July, one thousand seven hundred and ninety-three. Lat. 52° 20′ 48″ N." Mackenzie was knighted for his explorations, and in 1804 he was made the head of the North West Company.

The discovery of the western part of the continent was exciting the imagination of several nations more or less simultaneously. Lewis and Clark made their famous overland voyage in 1805, thus laying claim to the lands from the Missouri to the Columbia rivers in the name of the United States. The Russians, by way of Alaska, were working down the coast, and John Jacob Astor was establishing his company on the Pacific.

The North West Company was to send two more explorers westward, Simon Fraser and David Thompson. Fraser, not knowing of the Lewis and Clark Expedition, set forth in 1807, with orders from his company to reach the Columbia River. He found a mighty river, and followed it, but when he took his bearings, great was his disappointment, for it was too far north to be the Columbia River—thus we have the Fraser River. Thompson, also in 1807, reached the Columbia and spent four years exploring it, building posts and establishing the fur trade as he went. The boundary west of the Rocky Mountains was not settled until 1846, and in the meantime, under the joint ownership of Britain and the United States, the North West Company was actively engaged in fur trading there. (Astor sold his post in Astoria to the North West Company.)

It is interesting to notice the influence these explorers, in the name of the fur trade, had on the future of Canada. Had they not pushed westward and established claim to the land beyond the Rockies, it is possible that Canada today might not reach from ocean to ocean.

The North West Company had established itself successfully against its rival, the Hudson's Bay Company. Its trading posts dotted the map from Lake Superior to the Columbia River. However, from a different source came trouble to unsettle their success. They attributed this new trick of fate to spiteful revenge on the part of their rival. Actually the cause was very different.

Lord Selkirk, a Scottish nobleman, was much distressed by the pitiful condition of many of the people in the Highlands of Scotland who had lost their little farms when sheep raising was introduced. He conceived the idea of making it possible for them to obtain another start in the colonies. He first located two groups, one in Prince Edward Island, and the other in Upper Canada, but in order to carry out his plans on a large scale, he required plenty of land in the West. This could be done only through one of the two rival companies. Now it happened that the Hudson's Bay Company's stock was falling. Business had not been too good in the past few years because of the loss of the French market due to the Napoleonic Wars. Selkirk bought up a large block of this stock and then made his proposition to the company, which voted to give him the land he desired. The grant on the Red River lay about equally in what is now the province of Manitoba, and the present states of Minnesota and North Dakota. (The international boundary between the Lake of the Woods and the Rockies was not established until 1818.)

A glance at the map will prove instantly that a farming settlement in this area would play havoc with the trade of the North West Company. Settlers came out from Scotland in 1812, and endured frightful hardships in order to establish their little community. For five years they lived in constant terror of the métis. Selkirk, hearing of their plight, crossed the ocean to come to their assistance. He expended over half a million dollars on the colony and, before leaving, he negotiated the first Indian treaty of the Canadian Northwest.

Ironically enough, Selkirk's death in 1820, helped his colony more than anything he did during his lifetime. While he lived, the rivalry between the two companies flourished. Less than a year after he died, a merger was arranged whereby the Hudson's Bay Company bought out the North West Company. The entire business was reorganized and, for Montreal, the days of the fur trade were gone forever.

As the decades of the nineteenth century passed, and the population grew, discontent became evident. The people were unhappy about their government, and they became determined to do something about it. In this movement we see the seeds planted by the American Revolution beginning to take root. Not that there was widespread demand for independence, but rather that citizens wanted to have their rights as British subjects.

Now the American Revolution had taught the British government two lessons. One was that they must not let colonies develop practically free of control, and the other, that any taxation must be done by the colonies themselves. With these two cardinal principles in mind, the London government set up the Constitutional Act of 1791. Each of the colonies was given an elective assembly, with the power to make laws and to tax themselves. However, that lawmaking power was not to be allowed to have free rein. Three checks were made to guarantee against this—the council, then the governor, and lastly the home government in London. The governor ruled with the advice of the council whom he could appoint and dismiss at will, while he, in turn, was answerable to the government in London.

The system worked while the colonies were weak, but as they grew up it failed to satisfy them. The executive department had become too firmly entrenched. What had happened was this. When the governments of the colonies were established, it was difficult to find men with sufficient education and ability among the settlers. Once they were found, they became invaluable, and served on from year to year. This was not true of the governor who almost always was a military officer from England, or from some similar post elsewhere. His tenure of office varied with his success or failure, but, in any case, the man holding that post was a stranger and forced to lean on the resident officials for advice. We can see that such information as London had of the colonies was secured indirectly from this group of permanent office holders and, in the long run, they directed the policy of the government. Legally they were responsible to the governor, but actually they were indispensable to him.

As the colonies grew, so did the demand for the form of self-government similar to that operating in Britain. The Reformers who advocated this change wanted an executive chosen from the legislature and responsible to it—responsible government. Such an executive would remain their leader while he carried out the wishes of the majority of the people's representatives, the legislature.

London opposed this movement, as did the ruling clique of each province. Both believed that the majority of the people could not be entrusted with control of public affairs, and that responsible government would mean independence. If the executive were responsible to the legislative assembly, chosen by the people, how could the same man be responsible to the London government? The agitation was most severe in Upper and Lower Canada where the executive authority was more completely entrenched. In the former province the dominating group came to be known as the "Family Compact," in the latter, as the "Château clique."

In Lower Canada the problem of government was complicated by the race issue. The English minority who had moved into the province after 1763, had worked for an assembly, but when they got it in 1791, and at the same time found themselves separated from Upper Canada, they were in a hopeless minority. In desperation they made a complete about face, denounced popular government and rallied around the ruling group, for it was composed chiefly of their own kinsmen. This Château clique developed a strong anti-French policy.

Meanwhile the French were slow to learn the value of the Assembly. They had had no previous experience with such an institution. When they finally realized what they had, they became aware that the council and the government was being managed by the Château clique, hostile to them in every respect. Thus began a struggle for control of the expenditures of the province, and for an elective council which would include adequate French representation. A deadlock ensued; progress stopped. Governor after governor was sent out to deal with the situation, but without success. From the French ranks arose a fiery orator, Louis Joseph Papineau. As the years passed he became increasingly radical. So great was his popularity that as a member of the assembly for twenty-four years, he was, with one exception, always chosen as its speaker. He grew so offensive to the governor that the latter refused to accept his re-election to that office. The idea of armed resistance began to gain supporters, and soon both sides were quietly making preparations. Once again, the Roman Catholic Church stepped in, as it had at the time of the American Revolution and during the War of 1812. Although it was fearful of minority rule, it was more fearful of Papineau's influence on the people. When revolt came in 1837, certainly fewer French Canadians supported it than would have otherwise. Two uprisings occurred, but were quickly crushed, and Papineau fled to the United States—without leading the fight he had started.

In Upper Canada there was no racial conflict, but there were problems a-plenty. As a landlocked province, it was dependent upon either Lower Canada or the United States to ship in goods from the outside world. Import duties were collected at their point of entry, namely Lower Canada or the United States. Upper Canada recovered a part of what was collected on the St. Lawrence, but not a just share. At the same time, roads, bridges, and canals were necessary. Canals, especially, were indispensable to commerce, because of the rapids and falls that otherwise obstructed water transportation. Upper Canada in trying to provide these, became nearly bankrupt, and the government was blamed.

The land problem was also a source of annoyance. When the province was created, one-seventh of every township was set aside for the support of the Church (Church of England), and one-seventh for the support of the government. These lands remained undeveloped, and prevented continuous settlement. The building and maintenance of roads, schools, and churches, became a great burden to the taxpayers. To add insult to injury, many friends and relatives of government officials seemed to hold generous grants for speculation. Although the people of Upper Canada were overwhelmingly Protestant, all were not members of the Church of England, yet that denomination claimed all land reserved for religious support in each township. Even after the population had become predominately Methodist and Presbyterian, the Church of England still maintained its right to these "clergy reserves."

The members of the Family Compact, though they were not all blood relations, were Loyalists and frequently members of the Church of England. They ruled Upper Canada with an iron hand. The elective assembly, finding itself to be little more than a debating society, demanded the right to an elective council in which they could gain membership, and to control over the spending of the public revenue.

In Upper Canada, the leader of the popular cause was William Lyon MacKenzie, grandfather of the present Prime Minister, a rabble rouser, a born agitator, whose force in attacking his opponents was augmented by means of his newspaper, the *Colonial Advocate*. He so enraged the Family Compact that five times he was expelled from the legislative assembly, and five times overwhelmingly re-elected. His persecution by the Tory group won him the popular acclaim of the province. Naturally, with similar events occurring in Lower Canada, MacKenzie and Papineau began to correspond, and to plan for joint action.

There might have been no uprising in Upper Canada had the lieutenant governor not withdrawn the garrison to aid the authorities of Lower Canada. Toronto, unguarded, with a considerable store of arms and ammunition, was too much of a temptation for MacKenzie and his followers. He rallied about five hundred people for a march on the city. They were met by a force of citizens, more than twice as strong, and retired. Two days later another futile stand was made, and then MacKenzie also fled to the United States.

The rebellions, though unsuccessful, aroused London to the

need for decisive action. Lord Durham, one of the outstanding British statesmen, was dispatched to the colonies in 1838, with wide powers to take charge of the whole situation in British North America. Although he stayed in Canada only five months, Durham gained an amazing insight into the colonial problem. His report, submitted to the Crown, was a sweeping condemnation of the whole system of government, the meddlesome interference of the British Foreign Office, the graft, the lack of education, and the absence of local government. His solution for the colonial problem was to give the people liberty, equal to that enjoyed by citizens in Britain. He advocated a federation of British North America. He urged the union of Upper and Lower Canada under one government. In this last proposal, once again, we see expressed the vain hope that some day French nationalism would disappear if only both races were to mingle freely. Even he, astute as he was, failed to recognize the vitality of the French Canadian.

Durham's Report has become one of the beacon lights of Canadian history. However, its fame is one which has gradually grown with the passage of time. It certainly was not hailed as a masterpiece when he submitted it.

The British government acted on the report to the extent of joining Upper and Lower Canada. The Union Act of 1840 was very unfair to the French. English was made the only official language. Upper and Lower Canada, now to be known as Canada West and Canada East, were to be united in one legislature, each to hold an equal number of seats, though the population of the former was considerably less. The debts of the two provinces were merged, and Canada East was saddled with the burden that Canada West had accumulated. Responsible government, as proposed by Durham, was shelved for the time being. However, the British government did uproot one of the injustices, notably permanent tenure of office. This got rid of the small, influential, governing cliques which had been the cause of so much trouble.

It eventually became evident that half measures were doomed to failure. The one province in which there was no discord was New Brunswick. The reason for this was the need for British support because of the unsettled boundary with Maine. The St. Croix River dispute came to a head, and what is known as the Aristook War broke out in 1838-39. Lumbermen from both sides clashed. Soon American and British troops were called in. Fortunately, a truce was arranged and a decision reached in the Webster-Ashburton Treaty of 1842. The land in dispute was divided between both claimants. The fact that neither side was satisfied with the decision is perhaps proof that it was a fair one.

CHAPTER XI

◇◇ *The Dominion in the Making* ◇◇

To RETURN TO THE STORY of the struggle for responsible government, London at last decided to give the colonists what they wanted. In 1847, Lord Elgin was sent out to inaugurate the new system. Elgin was a firm believer in responsible government, and he determined to do his utmost to make the system work. Unlike Durham, who by the way was his father-in-law, he realized that the French Canadians would never lose their identity. Consequently, he persuaded the government to restore the use of the French language in the legislature, and when a deadlock occurred, he called in two leaders, French and English, to form an administration. Of course the English element were incensed at Elgin's action, and it was not long before they found a ready weapon with which to attack him. For some time there had been talk of the justice of repaying such people as had suffered property loss through the rebellion of 1837. When the government finally introduced the Rebellion Losses Bill in 1849, the fight was on. The Tories accused the government of putting a premium on treason, and clamored for a veto by the governor. Elgin, true to the principles of responsible government, signed the bill after it had been passed by the assembly. The Tories forgot caution and adopted the violence they had previously professed to abhor. A mob burned the Parliament buildings, wrecked property and hurled missiles at the governor's carriage as he drove through the streets of Montreal. (Montreal would probably be the capital of the nation had it not been for this disgraceful outburst of violence.)

Following this demonstration, many prominent businessmen of Montreal banded together to draw up the Annexation Manifesto.

Partly due to rage against Elgin, but more on account of economic reasons, annexation to the United States was thought to be desirable. A list of some nine hundred names were obtained, French as well as English.

Why did these people turn to union with the United States? Britain had adopted free trade in 1846. To the colonies this meant economic emancipation, but they lost a preferential place in British markets. They were now face to face with open competition in the world market. The Montreal merchant saw ruin ahead. Union with the United States would provide markets for Canadian goods. However, the Annexation Manifesto brought no answering welcome from across the border. At that point in its career, the United States was too concerned with settling the problem of Texas and California, to risk the addition of more potential "free" states into the Union. Lord Elgin, realizing that Canadian business was suffering because of free trade, sought another solution to the problem. He visited Washington and entered negotiations which resulted in the Reciprocity Treaty of 1854. This treaty provided a free market for the principal exports of Canada and the Maritime Provinces. Prosperity returned, and a few years later the Canadians realized that two could play at the game of regulating trade. If Britain could do it, so could they under their new system of responsible government. Loud were the protestations in England when, in 1859, a protective tariff act was passed. English manufacturers appealed to the government, the government remonstrated with Canada, but to no avail. With annexation but a few years in the past, it was evident that the colonies would go their own way, without, if not within, the Empire.

The Dominion of Canada came into existence in 1867, two years after the close of the Civil War. The idea of a federal union was not a new one. It had been suggested in the years following the American Revolution. At that time, distance, together with the weakness of each of the several colonies, made the idea impractical. Later, in 1838, Lord Durham realized that a prosperous and self-reliant British North America would come only through a union of all the provinces, but still the plan was considered premature.

By the middle of the nineteenth century, a number of circumstances conspired to bring together the provinces of British North America. The railway, already in use over short distances, seemed a possible means of linking the scattered provinces. Canada East and West had been joined together, and a branch line to Portland, Maine, gave an outlet to the ocean. The Maritimes had three small railways. A long connecting link from Canada East into the Maritimes would pull those two areas together.

As Canada West expanded, the newcomers were obliged to accept much less desirable land. The forested rocks of the Canadian Shield to the north, discouraged expansion in that direction. From then on, new settlers turned southward across the Great Lakes, into the United States Middle West. Immigrants still poured into Canada, but kept on through, across the international border. Canada needed a West for her own expansion.

Now at a very opportune time, the Hudson's Bay Company was losing its grip over its western holdings. It had built up a mighty fur empire to the Pacific, and had successfully ousted competition. In due course, Americans had settled in Oregon and desired to be included in the United States, so some permanent arrangement of the boundary was essential. Unable to settle the boundary west of the Rockies in 1818, both the United States and Britain had agreed to joint ownership. In the United States many people were demanding that the government annex the entire western coast as far north as Alaska. The slogan, "Fifty-four, Forty or Fight," won an election in 1844. However, by mutual agreement in 1846, the forty-ninth parallel was carried through the mountains to the sea. Though the problem seemed settled, the rapidity with which American expansion was progressing convinced many Canadian leaders that sooner or later, if the land north of the

forty-ninth parallel remained unsettled, Americans would overflow into it, and Canada would lose it.

What was to happen to British North America? If not united
could the separate colonies survive? Widely separated by barriers
that seemed impassable, they were strung out for hundreds of
miles along the northern boundary of the United States. The
Maritimes were separated from Canada East and West by the
mountainous area in the north of New Brunswick, Canada East
and West from the Red River by hundreds of miles of rocks and
forests; the Pacific was completely cut off—fifteen hundred miles
from the Red River, with the Rockies intervening.

The four separate sections of British North America were in
closer contact, geographically, commercially, and socially, with the
American states to the South than with each other. Canada traded
with New York and Portland, Maine, by rail. The Maritimes still
used the sea for trade with New England, but there was talk of a
rail line through southern New Brunswick to Portland, Maine.
The Red River Colony had found an outlet through Minnesota,
and British Columbia was far more closely in touch with California than with Canada or the Maritime Provinces.

In the Maritimes, especially, each province had its own history
and its own traditions. Provincialism was strong. With Canada
they had had little or no dealings, and thus there were no ties to
draw them together. Empire builders talked boldly of telegraph
and railway lines across the continent, but the people as a whole
were still to be convinced. How soon they were to be forced into
a decision they little knew.

In 1861 the Civil War broke out in the United States. Though
the "underground railway" had carried many a Negro slave to
freedom in Canada in the years before the war, and though Britain
had abolished slavery nearly thirty years earlier, a number of un-
forseen circumstances conspired to put both Britain and British
North America in a bad position with the United States government. Now Canada was not entirely blameless throughout this

struggle. During the war the government of Britain was partial to the Southern cause, and Halifax and Saint John became notorious bases for Southern blockade runners. In addition, the Canadian border swarmed with Confederate plotters who on one occasion, in 1864, descended on St. Albans, Vermont, looted three banks, rifled the vaults, started fires, and then made their way back to Montreal. Add to this the famous Trent Affair and the Alabama Claims Case, and one can readily see that with the close of hostilities in 1865, the United States had ample grounds should she chose to settle her score with Great Britain and British North America—and the provinces knew it.

The Union Act of 1840 had put Canada East and West under one government, with equal representation from each province. That had been very satisfactory to Canada West as long as the population of Canada East was larger. As time passed however, Canada West grew at a faster rate, and then the people demanded "Representation by Population"—shortened to "Rep. by Pop." To the French who had agreed to the arrangement when they had the greater population, this seemed grossly unfair. The English and the French, two races, separated by religion, customs, tradition, and geography, were thrown together to work out one government. Every cabinet had to have two heads, and two halves, one from Canada East and the other from Canada West. In addition, it had to have the support of each half of the legislature, because neither half would stand for rule by the other. It is perfectly clear that such a condition could not go on indefinitely. By 1864 the situation had become desperate. Within three years there had been two elections and three cabinets. Government was virtually at a standstill.

Meanwhile, negotiations for a connecting link of railway with Canada East broke down, and the three provinces decided to consider a local union which would include Nova Scotia, New Brunswick, and Prince Edward Island. Plans were made for a conference at Charlottetown in 1864. At that point the Canadian

Coalition government asked permission to send delegates. They were cordially received, and so well did they state their case for federal union that the conference was adjourned to meet again at Quebec, less than a month later.

In Quebec, the plan of union, now the basis of Canada's constitution, was worked out. The delegates agreed to the immediate need for a railroad to connect the Maritimes with Canada East and to the incorporation of the Northwest and of British Columbia as soon as possible. On the question of money the convention almost split up. It was proposed that the national government should control the tariff. The Maritimes were unwilling to lose the revenue. A compromise was finally worked out that provided for the payment to each province of an annual grant of money from the Dominion treasury in lieu of separate tax collections.

To get the consent of the several colonies was the next task. The leaders recognized the danger of delay, but were the people aware of it? Once again, as on three previous occasions, the Roman Catholic Church came to the rescue. The church leaders saw that the alternative to federation might well be annexation by the United States. They considered their existing racial and religious privileges under the British system preferable to the unimportant and insignificant position which would probably be their lot as part of a rapidly expanding United States. The people of the Maritimes were doubtful of the desirability of federation. They had less reason to fear the United States, for they had the support of the British Navy. In addition, they were not too sure that their wishes would carry sufficient weight in view of the larger population in Canada East and West. Britain exerted pressure to promote the cause of union, and the United States, at this point, by denouncing the Reciprocity Treaty of 1854, drove the provinces into federation as a substitute for the loss of American markets.

Events moved quickly. Representatives from Canada East and West, New Brunswick, and Nova Scotia gathered in London to draw up the British North America Act, on the basis of the Quebec Resolutions. Two months saw the work completed, and the bill ready for Parliament. This act was unique. Though planned in consultation with the British government, it was the work of the colonies themselves. As a name for the new country "The Kingdom of Canada" was proposed, but as the British government thought it might offend the republic to the south, "The Dominion of Canada" was substituted in its place.

Canada began its history as a nation in 1867, with four provinces, Nova Scotia, New Brunswick, Quebec (Canada East) and Ontario (Canada West). The Dominion was then only one tenth its present size. The Hudson's Bay Company still owned vast tracts of land in the north and west.

Canada had been hopeful of obtaining the West without paying for it. However, in 1866, when the American Congress debated a bill to annex the land north of the forty-ninth parallel, and when Senator Sumner of Massachusetts suggested that the Alabama Claims might be settled simply by annexing British North America, it was decided that speed was essential. Canada hastened to purchase the western lands from the Hudson's Bay Company. The Red River Colony became the Province of Manitoba in 1870, British Columbia joined the Dominion in 1871, and Prince Edward Island, in 1873.

The simplest method of understanding the government of Canada is to contrast it with that of the United States. The Constitution of the United States defines and explains the American system. The British North America Act does somewhat the same for Canada. Canada, like the United States, has a two-house legislature, the Senate and the House of Commons. In the United States the members of both houses are elected by the people; in Canada, the House of Commons represents the people, while the members of the Senate are appointed for life by the Governor-General. (This means that, in practice, they are chosen by the Prime Minister.)

The Governor-General, appointed by the Crown, upon the recommendation of the Ottawa government, is the King's representative in Canada. He acts upon the advice of the Dominion government, as does the King in Britain—to call Parliament into session, to adjourn or dissolve it, and to sign all bills passed by the legislature.

The Prime Minister of Canada corresponds to the President of the United States. He remains chief executive only for so long as he has the support of a majority of the members of the House of Commons. In the United States, the legislature and the President hold office for fixed periods of time; people know when elections will be held. In Canada, the members of the House of Commons and the Prime Minister hold office up to five years, but at any time, if the majority in that body vote down a bill proposed by their chief executive and his cabinet, it becomes time to find out by election which group the voters of the Dominion favor.

Canada, like the United States, has two traditional parties, the Liberal Conservative (now called Progressive Conservative), and Liberal. The Prime Minister, himself a member of the House of Commons, is the leader of the party which gained the largest number of seats in the previous election. He chooses his cabinet from members of the legislature. The actions of the cabinet members are subject to the will of the majority in the House of Commons. When the Prime Minister and his cabinet fail to win the approval of that body, as expressed in a majority vote, they resign, and two alternative courses of action are possible. The leader of the Opposition, (the political party which does not have a majority of seats in the House of Commons), may be asked to form a cabinet and carry on the government, or, more frequently, parliament is dissolved and an election called.

In the United States the three departments of the government are separated. In Canada, the legislative and the executive departments are interwoven. The Prime Minister and his cabinet— the executive officials—are also legislators. They sit in Parliament, debate, and propose legislation.

The Constitution of the United States provides that all "powers not delegated to the United States by the Constitution, nor prohibited by it to the States, are reserved to the States or to the people." Canada, organized at the close of the Civil War, profited from the example of that bloody conflict by providing more specifically for the division of powers between the federal and the provincial governments. For example, the British North America Act gives the Dominion government the right to appoint or to remove lieutenant-governors. (The provinces have lieutenant-governors, instead of governors.) Also, it may disallow provincial laws within one year of their passage. To make doubly certain that the division of power is clearly marked, the Act enumerates the powers of both the provincial and the federal governments, and gives to the federal government—"all matters not . . . assigned exclusively to the Legislatures of the Provinces."

The United States has both state and federal courts. Laws made by the state government are punishable in state courts, and federal laws are punishable in federal courts. In Canada there is one system of criminal law for the entire Dominion. Each province has its own civil law. With the exception of the lowest courts, all judges are appointed and paid by the federal government. Civil law tends to be uniform, with the exception of the Province of Quebec where the use of the French code is guaranteed.

The Supreme Court of Canada, as the highest court in the land, hears appeals, both civil and criminal, and may give advice to Parliament upon request. (Students of government in the United States have suggested the desirability of providing such a plan for that country.) One higher court, the Judicial Committee of the Privy Council, sits in London, and is the highest tribunal in the Commonwealth and Empire. Although cases may be appealed to that body from the Supreme Court of Canada, criminal cases are no longer taken to London, and the function of that court has been confined to interpreting the British North America Act.

CHAPTER XII

❖❖ *Making Union Work* ❖❖

CANADA BEGAN HER CAREER as a nation under the leadership of John A. Macdonald. As the most prominent of the Fathers of Confederation, he quite naturally became her first Prime Minister. The story of Canada, therefore, becomes the story of Sir John A. Macdonald until his death in 1891. (He was knighted on the first Dominion Day, 1867.)

Macdonald was born in Scotland and brought by his parents to Upper Canada as a small boy. Forced to leave school at fifteen in order to help support the family, he studied law the hard way— in the office of a law firm. He became a brilliant man and an eminent statesman. He fought hard to achieve union for Canada, and he fought equally hard to make that union successful. Though he was not a great orator, his humor, wit, and persuasiveness combined to make his speeches well-nigh irresistible, and as a parliamentary debater in later years he was unrivalled. He inspired not merely the devotion of his own party, but drew to his side many of his opponents, until he could well have the satisfaction of knowing that almost every leading political figure once his adversary, became his friend. Nothing shows more clearly the esteem in which he was held than the expressions of tribute made upon his death in 1891. A funeral service in Westminster Abbey, attended by all ranks and classes of Englishmen from the Sovereign downward, was the first of its kind in honor of a Dominion statesman. In his memory, a tablet was erected in St. Paul's Cathedral, London, and his widow was elevated to the peerage with the title, Baroness Macdonald of Earnscliffe.

As we have seen, the provinces which united to form the Dominion of Canada were separated by distances so great that union was little more than an empty figure of speech. The only means of railroad connection between Quebec and the Maritime Provinces was through Portland, Maine; while to reach Manitoba, passengers and freight were forced to journey from Ontario to Chicago, on to St. Paul, and then northward. When British Columbia entered the union, a journey of three weeks, via ship and American railroads, was necessary in order to get from there to Ontario. Such isolated units could never hope to prosper, or to develop national feeling. The amazing growth and expansion of the United States continued to offer tantalizing opportunities which yearly drew thousands of settlers from Canada, and was making havoc of her growth.

Perhaps in Canada more than in any country in the world, railways have performed the function of linking the scattered population together, and of creating a bond of union. The price Nova Scotia demanded for joining the Dominion was a railroad to connect the province with Quebec. In addition, the Dominion had promised British Columbia a completed railroad in ten years. Sir John A. Macdonald originally planned to construct the western road on the same basis as that through New Brunswick to Nova Scotia, as a public service, but the difficulties involved so frightened his colleagues that it was decided to pay a private company to build and operate the road. The Canadian Pacific Railway Company was organized. To that company the government gave the sections of road already built, some seven hundred miles, $25,000,000 in cash, 25,000,000 acres of land in the fertile belt, as well as the promise of a twenty-year monopoly of western traffic. Although the price paid by the government seemed high, the need for a railway was imperative, and the terms had to be attractive if people were to be persuaded to invest in such a venture.

The United States unwittingly helped the cause of unity in Canada. Each of the provinces, like the states in the Union before 1789, had its own individuality. They had long been separated by great geographical distances, travel was rare, and suspicion easily aroused. The first problem with the United States came soon after the organization of the Dominion. It was the troublesome fisheries question. We referred previously to the agreement of 1818 under which Americans were permitted to share the coastal fishing privileges off Newfoundland, Labrador, and the Magellan Islands. However, their right to fish along the coast of any other part of British North America was cancelled. Americans could enter any harbor for shelter, wood, water, or repairs, but on no account for fishing, curing, or drying. Years passed, and it was found that the mackerel, formerly abundant along the New England coast, had moved northward. The American fishermen followed, to the tune of many disputes. With reciprocity in 1854, the problem ceased, because that treaty had opened inshore fishing to Americans. When the United States cancelled the Reciprocity Treaty in 1866, however, the fishermen kept on plying their trade without rights. The Canadian government tried to enforce licensing, but the fishermen cared little for such technicalities. Then the former took a decisive step. All foreigners were excluded from the coastal waters and a small fleet of cruisers was sent to enforce the law. The United States finally agreed to pay indemnities to the value of $5,500,000, and the inshore fisheries were opened to American vessels for ten years. The treaty was a severe disappointment to Canada. What rankled with the Canadian public, and stirred national spirit, was the United States demand for fishing rights and at the same time their refusal to consider reciprocity.

It was Canada's intention to avoid the problem still plaguing the United States, namely trouble with the Indians. With this in mind, Ottawa laid plans to prepare the Northwest Territories for the arrival of white settlers, and to stop the influence of the American "Wild West" from spreading across the boundary by organizing the North West Mounted Police in 1873. A thousand-mile boundary, undefended, made it all too easy for lawbreakers and smugglers to escape across the line, there once more to ply their trade. Already whiskey-laden wagons from America were corrupting the Indians of Canada, and the latter, numbering about 36,000, were becoming dangerous.

The North West Mounted Police, known since 1920 as the Royal Canadian Mounted Police, have made a name for themselves in the halls of fame. Three hundred men in all conquered the West, established law and order, and made that wilderness safe for settlers. Their success is explained by the rigorous qualifications necessary for admission. It was a hand-picked group, strong in body, of superior education and intelligence. Though a civilian organization, it has not been uncommon for its officers to hold military rank.

When the police arrived in the West their presence was felt at once. Without waiting to provide shelter for themselves, they began to round up whiskey smugglers. The Indians were quick to see that these men were there to protect their interests. In a short time the way was cleared for making treaties with the tribes in anticipation of the settlers soon to arrive. The government promised a yearly payment of money to the Indians, and reserved lands for their use, where no whites could settle—a square mile for every family of five. In addition, the Indian received farming implements, cattle, and any other necessary assistance.

It was none too soon. Indians in the United States were urging their northern brethren to join in the fight to oust the white man. After the American government retaliated against the defeat of General Custer, Sitting Bull and several thousand Sioux retreated across the border. The situation was tense, and trouble could have developed had the "Mounties" not been on such good terms with the Canadian Indians. In Eastern Canada the newspapers and the people were panic stricken at the thought of the bloodthirsty Sioux, with only a few hundred police to control them. They urged that regiments of soldiers be sent to drive them out. To the amazement of Canadians as well as Americans, this small group of police handled the situation beautifully, rounded up the thousands of Sioux and returned them to the United States.

Friendship between the French and British Canadians is inclined to wear very thin when subjected to any unusual strain. We have already found that when Manitoba was being admitted to the Dominion, the government had not taken sufficient account of the settlers already there, with the result that the métis, under Louis Rièl, had resisted the absorption of the Red River Colony into the Union. When in that unfortunate episode an Ontario Orangeman was killed, that province cried out for the death of Rièl, and Quebec equally violently opposed it. Rièl's escape to the United States temporarily solved the situation.

The coming of the railway, the flocking in of settlers, and the disappearance of vast herds of buffalo—their chief support—made nomadic life no longer possible for the métis in the Northwest Territories. Those people had, of necessity, turned to agriculture. They had taken land, and laid out their farms according to the old French pattern—long narrow strips, two miles by one eighth of a mile—running back from the Saskatchewan River. When government men appeared to survey according to the well-known checkerboard pattern, they feared the loss of their holdings, and they requested the government to give them title to their lands. Although Canadians on the spot recognized the justice of their claims, the Dominion government was slow to act, and clerks were slower to carry out the policy finally agreed on by the government. Petition followed petition to Ottawa, delegation followed delegation, until finally, completely exasperated, the métis turned to Rièl. He arrived from Montana in 1885, where he had been living in exile, set up a rebel government, and encircled a party of North West Mounted Police and some volunteers, sent to dislodge him. Twelve men were killed. Militia, sent from the East soon crushed the rebellion, but Rièl was captured and condemned to death.

The government was in an awkward position. Rièl was a troublemaker and a murderer. The English-speaking population demanded his death; the French defended him. To Quebec, the rebellions in both the Red River Colony and along the Saskatchewan River represented the efforts of a minority group driven to revolt in order to obtain justice. The métis were French and, according to French Canadian reasoning, they were suffering from their English antagonists. Pressure from English-speaking Canada strong. The government could not ignore it. Rièl was executed. From that time, the French Canadian people began to turn against Macdonald and the Liberal-Conservative Party.

Although the governor-generalship had been created to act as a link between the British and Canadian governments, and all communications between London and Ottawa passed through his hands, the Canadian government in 1880, appointed a Canadian High Commissioner, in order to have a direct representative in London. In 1877, Britain agreed that, unless the Dominion wished to be included, no future commercial treaties made by London would be binding on Canada.

Many public men in England had contended, for several decades, that the Empire was bound to break up on account of free trade. When Canada became a dominion, they saw in that a step toward independence, and welcomed it. When, however, dominion status did not seem to be producing the results anticipated, a changed viewpoint became evident, and arguments were put forward for encouraging coöperation and partnership between the Dominion and the London government. Out of these later ideas came the first Colonial Conference in 1887, which was attended by Canada and every self-governing colony. While the immediate results were of no great importance, it marked the first of a series of conferences, later to play an important part in the development of the Empire.

Macdonald worked constantly to develop a truly Canadian policy. He tried to promote friendly relations with the United States, and at the same time to avoid extreme proposals which might lead to eventual annexation. He realized that Canadians possessed rights and freedom under British citizenship that offered a far greater advantage than they could hope to secure as a small independent nation. At the same time, he was determined that Canada should control her own affairs, in her own way, and that relations with Britain should be on a coöperative basis.

Wilfrid Laurier followed Macdonald as Prime Minister. He was a French Canadian, (the only one to become Prime Minister), and a Roman Catholic. More than any single individual, he brought the two races together in harmony. He loved the people of his own race, he loved Canada, and he was devoted to Britain. His simplicity and kindliness, his honesty and courtesy, his moderation and calmness, his tolerance and frankness, won the admiration and confidence of the English Canadians, and the adoration of the French.

Laurier is popularly remembered today as an orator. Without doubt he was the most effective public speaker Canada has produced. Erect, dignified, reserved, carefully groomed, he was a commanding figure in any gathering. He had an abundance of that natural courtesy and charm that is so characteristic of the French people. However, Laurier's claim to greatness rests on a foundation firmer than any that sheer oratory could produce. Perhaps the most outstanding feature of his public life was his moderation. Even in the heat of political combat he never lost for a moment his self-control. He might be caustic or even delicately satirical, but he never made personal remarks about his political opponents in order to win an election. He suffered the enmity of many leaders in his Church, but with it all he maintained a quiet respect for the faith into which he had been born, and at the same time, the dignity of his own opinions.

Unlike Macdonald, Laurier, though born to a family of only moderate means, had the advantage of a university education. While still a boy, his father sent him to live in a near-by town in order that he might learn the English language in an English Protestant school. There he made friends with a Scottish Presbyterian family to whom, in later life, he was wont to attribute his religious tolerance. There is little doubt that his mastery of the English langauge, and his consequent love of the literature of that country, greatly influenced his character and opinions. He recognized that English must be the language of commerce, politics, and literature, and that its mastery was essential if one was to participate effectively in the life of the nation.

While in England to attend Queen Victoria's Diamond Jubilee in 1897, he won the affection and admiration of the people in the British Isles. Oxford and Cambridge conferred honorary degrees upon him, and he was knighted by the Queen.

Laurier, when he became Prime Minister, inherited a bitter problem from the previous administration. Manitoba, when it was made a province, established a public educational system like that of Quebec, with two sets of schools, one English-speaking and Protestant, and the other French-speaking and Roman Catholic. Later immigration made Manitoba overwhelmingly an English-speaking province. In 1890 the provincial legislature abolished the separate schools and the use of the French language. In the name of the minority, Quebec objected, and demanded the restoration of the dual system. According to the constitution of Canada, the Dominion had power to disallow an act of a provincial legislature within one year. Laurier was faced with the thorny problem of either upholding Quebec's demand for a continuation of the dual school system in Manitoba, or of bowing to the will of the majority in the nation.

His decision was a fair one, although he did not reinstate the separate schools as the Roman Catholic Church urged. He recognized that Manitoba was Protestant, and that nothing would be gained, and much lost, if the people were forced against their own wishes to support two school systems. The plan he put into operation provided that in a single school system, for the last half-hour of the day, Protestants and Roman Catholics should be separated for religious instruction—if their parents wished it—and that any school, having a large enough minority of either French or English, should provide a teacher to carry on instruction in that tongue. This reasonable solution satisfied the great body of people throughout the country. However, his own Church leaders, bitter and hostile, demanded that good Catholics have nothing to do with the French Canadian leader or his party, that they must choose between "Christ and Satan." Laurier, although a devoted member of the Church, plainly expressed his view on the political authority any Church should wield. As citizens, the clergy were equally at liberty to express their political views, but the right of an individual, no matter how lowly, to think for himself was sacred and should never be influenced by the threat of clerical disfavor. The attacks upon Laurier by his own Church continued to be so bitter that a number of Roman Catholics appealed to the Vatican for papal intervention. Laurier's fearless stand, plus papal support, combined to end the open activity of the Roman Catholic clergy in Canadian politics.

Laurier was accused by his enemies of being more English than an Englishman. Such an accusation was absurd. However, he was devoted to the British system of government, and he saw great possibilities for the future of Canada, as a co-member of the British Empire. With this in mind, he originated the policy of preferential trade with England, later to be expanded by his successors of both parties, to include all the members of the British Commonwealth of Nations.

When the Boer War broke out in 1899, his government offered, and sent a Canadian contingent to South Africa—a precedent, and indicative of the fact that Canada was growing up. The pressure from British Canadians, on this question, was strong. French Canada was indifferent and, as far as a noisy minority was concerned, hostile. Laurier felt that he could not disregard the popular demand. As a result of his action we find the beginning of the French Canadian Nationalist movement in Canada—of which more later.

Early in Laurier's administrative career, one of the most difficult disputes in the history of United States-Canadian relations arose—that of the Alaskan boundary. As in the case of so many boundaries described in early treaties, the ignorance of geography made it impossible to fulfill the wording of the treaty. It made little difference to either the United States or to Canada for many years, but with the discovery of gold in the Yukon, in the 1890's, the definition of the boundary suddenly assumed vital importance. If the United States claim was valid, Canada had no sea coast north of 54° 40'. The section in dispute was that known as the "Panhandle." Canada proposed an arbitration board of three, but Theodore Roosevelt, then President of the United States, refused, and insisted, rather, on a commission of six, three men from each country. Canada agreed, with the stipulation that the members be "six impartial jurists of repute." When the appointments were announced, it was found that Great Britain and Canada had chosen three jurists as specified, while the United States had chosen three men, only one of whom could qualify for the description above, the other two were known to be opposed to Canada's claim—and not "impartial jurists." The American representatives would not compromise, so, to break the deadlock and to avoid trouble with the United States, the British member finally voted with the American delegates. The Canadians refused to sign the agreement, and, in Canada, the results when made known led to an outburst of popular feeling. Britain was accused of sacrificing Canada and of breaking faith.

The United States had exercised unchallenged control over the territory in dispute for thirty years. Although sections of the boundary could not be made to follow the exact wording of the treaty, there seems little doubt that in the main her claim was sound. Under the circumstances, she had nothing to lose by submitting the dispute to arbitration, or of rigidly adhering to her part of the phrase, "six impartial jurists of repute."

Laurier's prudence and restraint is nowhere better illustrated than in his dealings with the award of the Alaskan Boundary Tribunal. He could have exploited national sentiment, already running high. He was as disappointed as all Canadians, but if he could not promote closer relations with Britain, he would not be a party to agitations which might tend to divide the Empire. This dispute, so disheartening to good relations between the United States and Canada at the time, is doubly significant. It was the last boundary dispute, and the last unpleasant incident to occur between them. Several years later, in 1909, that age-old fisheries problem was referred to the Hague Tribunal and settled for all time, and, in the same year, an event of world importance took place—the establishment of the permanent International Joint Commission. Canada and the United States agreed that, in future, any problems arising along their common frontier would be referred to a commission of six members, three from each country, with complete authority to investigate and to settle all cases. In the intervening years, this body has never failed to find a solution, and in most cases the decision has been unanimous.

For many years the United States had turned a deaf ear to Canadian proposals for a reciprocal trade agreement. Finally, America began to see some value in the plan, and President Taft was promoting it. The treaty might well have been concluded had not Speaker "Champ" Clark remarked, "I am for it because I hope to see the day when the American flag will float over every square foot of the British North American possessions clear to the North Pole." In Canada, patriotism burst forth in all its glory. An election was called in 1911, and Laurier went down to defeat together with the reciprocity treaty.

Laurier had guided Canada through a period of unprecedented growth and prosperity. He encouraged immigration, commerce, industry, and agriculture. Canada, on the eve of the First World War, was largely the product of his competent policy. During his fifteen years in office nearly ten thousand miles of railway were built, and two new transcontinental lines constructed. No country with a corresponding population had ever provided comparable outlets for its commerce. Meanwhile, industries were expanding. Manufacturing became centered in Quebec and Ontario; the riches of northern Ontario were beginning to be developed; and within a few years, hard-rock mining was to become one of Canada's leading industries. The more or less universal agricultural pattern had already given way to specialization. Everywhere, people were drifting from the country to the city. The Prairie Provinces had become the granary of the nation, and to a large degree, of the world. By 1914, Canada had become a country of some importance. Her great days were still ahead, her resources were only beginning to be tapped, her population was increasing very satisfactorily, and she was taking her place as one of the export nations of the world.

CHAPTER XIII

⟡ *Canada Comes of Age* ⟡

THE FIRST WORLD WAR had far-reaching results for Canada. It marked the last turning point in the road to complete independence, economic and political. But first, a brief comment on Canada's place in the war effort, and on the great internal problem which the war created. Out of a population of less than eight million, she raised nearly 620,000 troops. Canadian soldiers were in the thick of the fighting, the first to be exposed to the effect of poison gas at Ypres on April 22, 1915, and to hold the line until reinforced four days later. Two thirds of her men were wounded and, from a population one twelfth that of the United States, she suffered almost an equal number of casualties. The war imposed a heavy burden of debt and a severe strain on her national unity.

Until 1917, enlistment was entirely on a volunteer basis. However, by that time it was apparent that replacements were not keeping up with casualties. The government, then under the leadership of Sir Robert Laird Borden, decided to introduce conscription. The French population opposed the plan. Laurier, as leader of the Opposition, was personally an enthusiastic supporter of the war effort, but he realized that his feelings were not shared by the majority of his fellow citizens of Quebec. Since the Boer War, many French Canadians had become increasingly alarmed at the degree to which Canada was being involved in European affairs. Henri Bourassa, the French Nationalist leader, was busily at work in an effort to undermine the unity between the races which Laurier had achieved, and to substitute in its place a strong French bloc. Bourassa had rallied around him all the discontented groups in the province of Quebec, and had wielded them into a political organization. On the basis of prejudice and racial antagonisms, it was not difficult to build such an organization, devoted to the perpetuation of French customs and institutions. Laurier felt that Parliament should not adopt conscription without referring the issue to the voters of the nation. He was confident that it would be overwhelmingly approved and that, on that basis, the French Canadians would acquiesce to the plan. The conscription controversy, however, split the Liberal Party. The great majority of the English-speaking members joined with the Conservatives to pass the Military Service Act, while the French members of the Party opposed it. Borden, at the behest of popular opinion, proposed a Coalition government (made up of members of both major parties) for the more successful and efficient prosecution of the war. He invited Laurier to join. The latter refused, if to do so involved the approval of conscription, for he felt that were he to join the Coalition cabinet he would lose much of his following in French Canada to Bourassa. A general election was called in 1917 and was bitterly contested. With minor exceptions, the vote was cast on racial lines. The government was sustained by reason of the fact that the English-speaking population outweighed the French, and the latter, showing good sense, bowed to public opinion.

Much has been spoken and written that accuses the French of not bearing their share in the war effort. The growing antagonism between the races became very marked during the war years, and was a serious threat to the unity of the country. It was evident that French recruits fell far behind those of British stock. Several logical reasons, often disregarded, accounted for this fact. For instance, the French married early. Their English counterparts were frequently still free from family ties, and therefore more available for service. Also, the French tie with Europe was very remote. Two hundred and fifty years had passed since their ancestors had migrated to the St. Lawrence. On the other hand, the English-speaking settlers were at most only a few generations removed from British soil; in 1914, nearly a million people in Canada had actually been born in the British Isles. In addition to this, an examination discloses the fact that native born Canadians of either origin lagged far behind those of British birth in rallying to the call of country. In the years prior to 1914, France had carried on an anticlerical campaign, which stirred the enmity of Roman Catholic leaders. Refugee French priests, arriving in Quebec, added voice to the already existent disapproval. To the devout population of French Canada, it seemed as though the war were God's judgment on France for her wickedness. As a result, any bond between the two peoples was broken. In addition, tactlessness on the part of the English-speaking population stirred resentment. It was hardly to be expected that French volunteers would rally to the call of a Protestant clergyman, backed by the Orange Order!—and that was exactly how recruitment was attempted in Quebec.

Robert Laird Borden is a difficult man to characterize; he had few of those qualities which attract publicity and make a man widely known. Born of Loyalist stock (his grandfather was one John Lathrop, of New Haven), on a farm in Grand Pré, Nova Scotia, he lived a quiet boyhood, became a teacher, and later studied law. He did not seek a political career, or particularly enjoy it. A quiet, dignified, reserved, unassuming man, a creditable scholar, and a prominent lawyer in Halifax, he found public life a burden, and only a stern sense of duty compelled him to endure it. As Prime Minister of Canada between 1911 and 1920, he guided the nation through a most difficult period. The last few years, during which he led the British Dominions toward a position of independence and equality with Britain, represent the crowning achievement of his public career.

Canada had been given a constitution and an independent parliament in 1867. She was still bound to Britain by a few ties, chief of which compelled her to conduct business with foreign nations through the London government. During the war, national feeling was aroused as it had never been before. The people could claim just pride in their achievements. They were not content with their present status. By a series of moves, Borden succeeded in gaining independence for Canada, and indirectly, in creating the British Commonwealth of Nations.

As he pointed out, Canada could not be expected to contribute half a million troops to the war effort without being given a voice in determining their distribution in the field and in the general war policy of the Empire. Lloyd George, when he took over the government of Britain in 1917, adopted Borden's proposal, and the prime ministers of all the Dominions were given seats in the Imperial War cabinet on equal terms with their British colleagues. In 1918, when the war policy of all the Allied nations was put under a single control, they took their places as members of the Supreme War Council of the Allies—their first direct contact with foreign governments. At the close of the war, Borden insisted that the Dominions had earned the right to be represented at the Peace Conference on the same basis as other small nations. As such, Canadian delegates attended the conference and signed the treaties, which were ratified later by the Canadian Parliament. When the League of Nations was formed, once more he demanded membership for Canada as an independent nation. It should be pointed out that Borden's efforts to achieve independence of action for the self-governing parts of the Empire, were misunderstood and resisted by other nations of the world. Opponents of the League of Nations in the United States criticized the fact that the British Empire would have several votes, while the United States would have only one.

In 1920 the way was paved for the direct exchange of ministers between the United States and Canada, and in 1927 a legation was established in Washington. Since then the field of diplomatic representation has been widened to include the major nations of the world, and most of the legations have become embassies.

The changed status of the Dominions within the Empire required a clearer definition of the relationship existing between them. The Balfour Declaration of 1926 and the Statute of Westminster in 1931, which created the British Commonwealth of Nations, recognized the Dominions as independent nations, equal in status to each other, and to Britain.

William Lyon MacKenzie King was appointed to the leadership of the Liberal Party, to succeed Sir Wilfrid Laurier, in 1919. They had been close friends, and the choice was a logical one, for King was widely recognized as one of the ablest of the younger Liberals. A graduate in political science and law from the University of Toronto, with advanced degrees from the universities of Chicago and Harvard, he had been well grounded in the theory of economics and government. He became vitally interested in labor conditions, and the welfare of the worker. King was invited by his government to organize the Department of Labor, and he soon acquired a reputation as a skillful mediator in the numerous industrial disputes which required solution. Throughout the First World War he was actively engaged in investigating and adjusting industrial disputes in the United States. His activities on behalf of labor have not ceased with his promotion to his present position. His championship of the workingman and his demand for democratic control of industry, reminds one of the bitter fight waged by his grandfather, William Lyon MacKenzie, against the vested interests of the Family Compact. Although there is much in his character that is akin to MacKenzie, the rebel, over it all there is a quietness, a moderation, a tactfulness, that has brought him a measure of success in his efforts to adjust inequalities, and to eliminate many of the conditions under which labor was forced to operate.

Canada's prosperity since the turn of the century had its origin in the rapid growth of the Prairie Provinces which, in turn, were dependent upon the markets of industrial Europe. With the outbreak of war, production in Europe declined and the demand became greater. It is little wonder that all who could, rushed into this profitable occupation. Farms were expanded and areas never intended for agriculture were put into production. The boom on the prairie was reflected throughout Canada. The eastern part of the country, in response to the demands of the western farmer, was developing into a great industrial area. Canada had never known such prosperity.

The return of peace eventually brought a readjustment in the agricultural market. Europe returned to the production of more of her own foodstuffs, and trade between countries slowed up. The war had put nations deeply into debt. They were not able to afford foreign trade, and many of them wished to build up an independent life by the old means of protecting their manufacturing from foreign competition. To Canada, whose people depended upon foreign markets in order to dispose of their surplus goods, this was disaster. It had been hoped that the flood of immigration might be resumed with the coming of peace, but gradually it became evident that such was not to be the case. Had immigration occurred, Canada would have been able to absorb more of the products which she produced, and this could have cushioned her fall.

The farmers of the West, finding it difficult to market their wheat, turned to coöperation in an effort to cut out the middleman. They organized the Pool—a central selling agency in each province to which all members entrusted the selling of their grain. The Pools built and bought a large number of grain elevators in the West, at the head of the Great Lakes, and on the ocean ports. They were well managed and very successful for a time—controlling over half the crop, they were among the biggest businesses in the world. Farmers who joined the Pool agreed to hand over all their wheat for a five-year period, at a down price of eighty cents per bushel. The Pools had full power to dispose of the wheat as they thought best, and the farmer received a second or even a third payment at the end of the fiscal year when the receipts were collected and the operating cost of the Pool known.

After 1929, however, the Pools could not sell their grain at the price advanced to the farmer. They went into debt. The provincial governments came to their aid, and finally the Dominion government took over the grain business. It set up the Wheat Board to receive and to sell wheat for such farmers as cared to use it, at a guaranteed price of 87½ cents per bushel. In addition, over a period of years, it managed to dispose of the tremendous surplus in the Pool.

One large industry which suffered from the war was the railroad. Expansion had been too rapid. Three transcontinental lines had been built at the expense of a heavy burden of debt. It had been thought that rail routes would carry the wheat directly to Quebec and the Maritimes for shipment to Europe. However, rail rates could not compete with the cheaper water route via the Great Lakes. Three transcontinental lines for a country of Canada's population meant keen competition. It became increasingly difficult to pay interest on the money borrowed for construction. The banks loaned as much as possible, and then the government had to come to the rescue with more loans. As a result, the railroads were hopelessly in debt. One by one they were forced into bankruptcy, until the Canadian Pacific alone remained.

The government took over all these insolvent railways plus their debts and reorganized them into the largest railway system in the world, the Canadian National Railway—for many years a liability, for the debt assumed by the government equalled the cost of the war. The government had little choice in the matter. It was faced with the prospect of going into the railway business or of permitting the credit of the country through its banks, to collapse, and it chose the former because that course would avoid disaster. Some people advocated selling the bankrupt companies to the Canadian Pacific, but that would have put the people at the mercy of a transportation monopoly. On the other hand, obviously, the government could not hope to obtain the money needful to purchase the Canadian Pacific—the national debt was already too great.

In 1929 the United States was plunged into a panic, probably the worst in her history. The depression which followed was reflected throughout the world. Canada suffered severely, though not to the degree experienced in the United States. Less highly industrialized, she had not experienced the phenomenal prosperity of the twenties, and her banking system, unlike that of the United States, was sound and able to bear the strain. The story of the attempts to overcome the depression in Canada is similar to that in the United States. Canadians reacted just as their cousins across the border—they blamed the government, and when the opportunity was presented, they turned it out. In 1930 the Conservatives were elected with Richard Bedford Bennett as Prime Minister. Bennett raised tariffs on the theory that by keeping out foreign competition, more Canadians would be employed. "Priming the pump" by means of public works, youth training projects (similar to the CCC), unemployment insurance, extension of credit to farmers, soil rehabilitation, and numerous other plans, served to increase the burden of national debt with little noticeable improvement. High tariffs were ruinous to Canada's export trade. All the provinces were staggering under the load of providing for the destitute, and the federal government had to come to their rescue.

The Liberals, returned to power by the same depression, in 1935, reversed the Conservative program. They lowered tariffs in order to increase trade with the outside world and negotiated a reciprocal trade agreement with the United States in 1935.

When the depression failed to lift, many people grew dissatisfied with the policies of the Liberals and Conservatives, and organized new political groups. One of these, the Social Credit Party, has never enjoyed much support outside the Province of Alberta. Its solution for the ills of the nation called for the abolition of banks, and for a monthly payment to each individual, on the order of the Townsend Plan. It won control of the Provincial government in

Alberta, completed the job of bankrupting the province, and ran afoul of the federal government.

The other party, Coöperative Commonwealth Federation, abbreviated to C.C.F., has sought to unite all workers, farmers, and the middle and professional classes on a program of state socialism. This program called for the socialization of all banking and certain industries, government regulation of imports and exports, of health, hospital and medical services. Although the C.C.F. has not yet succeeded in winning a federal election, it has become a national party, and its influence and policies are a matter of serious concern to both the Liberals and Conservatives. In Saskatchewan, the C.C.F. won control of the provincial legislature in 1944. As such, it has an opportunity to enforce the program of the party and thus to demonstrate to the nation the practicability which is claimed for it.

The conditions which produced the Social Credit Party and the C.C.F. were reflected in Quebec by a rising nationalist movement. In 1936 the Liberals, who had controlled the government for nearly half a century, were defeated by the newly organized Union Nationale. Duplessis, the leader of Union Nationale, was distrusted by all except his followers. He preached a brand of fascism, and he advocated race prejudice. There was talk of establishing a French Roman Catholic republic which would include not only Quebec but the part of New England inhabited by French Canadians. As the war clouds gathered, the racial strain became more evident. French Canadians were still isolationist. The Ethiopian crisis found the French lined up behind Mussolini. The Spanish Civil War produced a similar result, with French Canada supporting Franco. However, when Russia signed the pact with Hitler, the tension lifted, and upon the outbreak of war in Europe, the federal government voted unanimously to enter. Duplessis, unable to realize that Canada was united, brought on an election in Quebec. He made Canada's participation in the war the issue, and found himself badly trounced when the results of the balloting were announced.

In the decade prior to the German invasion of Poland, Canada, like the United States, was more concerned with her internal troubles. The problems created by the depression were affecting the life of all citizens. When they stopped to think about it, many people considered the rumblings from Asia and Europe to be no concern of theirs, and many more felt that the possibility of war was remote. Only a minority in both the United States and Canada sensed the impasse into which the world was drifting. When war broke out in 1939, Canada hesitated slightly. But it was soon evident to the people that, as an exporting nation, for one thing, they could not afford the possibility of German control of the sea lanes and the world markets. In addition, their mode of government, and their democratic institutions were in jeopardy, for all examples of Nazi domination had pointed to one irrevocable fact —death to democracy. So, on September 10, 1939, Canada, the first American nation to do so, entered the Second World War.

Although she was prepared to assume much greater responsibilities than in 1914, we must avoid falling into the error of comparing at first glance, Canada's contribution with that of the United States—a nation of twelve times the potential manpower.

When Canada declared war she had virtually no armament works, no production of large ships and large planes, no guns, no tanks. During the war years her factories more than doubled production. Great Bear Lake produced the uranium necessary for the atom bomb; Shipshaw was constructed; and the aluminium company plant in Arvida expanded to become the largest of its kind in the world.

The British Commonwealth Air Training Plan became Canada's greatest single contribution to the war. When it was fully developed, airmen from many parts of the British Commonwealth —and Americans, Poles, Dutch, Belgians, Czechs, and Free French as well—were trained in the hundred and fifty odd air and ground schools scattered throughout the Dominion. Seventy-one per cent of the staff, and more than half of the graduating airmen were Canadians. In addition, many veteran pilots of civilian air lines took over the task of ferrying American bombers across the Atlantic from Newfoundland to the British Isles, in the years before the United States entered the war.

The Canadian Navy undertook the protection of the North Atlantic convoy route, and she was responsible for almost all of the close escort duty between North America and the United Kingdom. She provided about a third of the support forces in the Atlantic; she participated in the evacuation of Dunkerque, in the Caribbean, and in the Mediterranean.

Mutual Aid is Canada's term for what Americans know as Lend-Lease. Prior to the passage of the act in 1943, Canada provided Britain with money to the value of about $2,700,000 to be used to purchase war supplies in Canada.

In August, 1940, President Roosevelt and Prime Minister King met and arranged for a Permanent Joint Board of Defense. This Odgensburg Agreement, as it is known, is significant because it marks a milestone in United States foreign policy—America had signed a permanent military agreement. Briefly, it will be remembered that after France fell, Britain alone barred Germany's path to the Western Hemisphere. Iceland, Greenland, and the West Coast of Africa all could be steppingstones to North America. Thus we see the reason for the agreement. An economy of effort was needed if the defenses of North America were to be completed. The Permanent Joint Board of Defense made plans for a network of air and naval bases and for the construction of necessary military highways. The following year, by the Hyde Park Declaration, Canada and the United States agreed that "each country should provide the other with the defense article which it is best able to produce. . . ." A joint committee took the responsibility for organizing and distributing the raw material resources of both countries, and arranged for a means whereby information could be readily exchanged across the border.

CHAPTER XIV

❧ *Canada Faces the Future* ❧

LITTLE DID ANYONE imagine in 1918 that some twenty years later Canada would replace France as a major participant in a second world war. Not only did the apparently impossible happen, but she became Britain's chief ally in the months following the retreat from Dunkerque. During six years of war she pushed ahead to take fourth place among the United Nations, to become the leading spokesman for the so-called "Middle Powers," and the largest contributor to UNRRA.

In the feeding of Europe's hungry, Canadians have taken a leading role—and one that demonstrates an exceptionally high sense of duty toward their fellow men. They could have removed rationing soon after hostilities ended. It was a temptation. But they chose to retain wartime controls and to observe the two "meatless days" each week. Although it is now over a year since the Japanese surrender, rationing continues as it did throughout the war.

Today, Canadians find themselves very much in the center of two international problems. As the major source of uranium for the atom bomb, they share responsibility for its ultimate fate. Also, they are very much concerned with their strategic location on the airways of the world, should Europe and America become involved in another war.

Take a globe and plot the most direct route from New York, Chicago, or San Francisco, to the important cities of Europe or Asia, and you will readily recognize the significance of Canada's position, and the reason for her vital interest in a permanent peace. The Northland has become an international frontier of importance not only to herself but to the United States.

The importance of the Arctic came as an appalling realization. Canadians became aware that they knew relatively little about their "new" frontier of thousands of miles. Extensive areas had never been penetrated by white men, had never even been observed from the air. Could a large group of men live in these regions, and be kept supplied with necessary provisions and reinforcements? How would machinery hold up in sub-zero temperatures?—and how could it be repaired? What clothing offers the best protection and yet allows a person to move about easily? What foods provide a maximum of nourishment with a minimum of bulk? These were some of the questions that confounded Canadians as they thought of the possibility of that dreadful day when war might descend unannounced from the empty North.

The people are taking a serious view of their responsibility to protect this new North American frontier. In an effort to begin to gain information, a large expedition of soldiers, scientists, and observers, known as Operation Musk Ox, set out last year to study winter conditions in the Northland. They travelled over vast expanses of snow and ice, they camped, built fires, studied weather conditions, endured tremendous hardships, and returned with much valuable data for government and military authorities.

Canada relies on foreign markets to a greater degree than any other nation. She depends on foreign customers for over a third of her national income; she is the world's leading export nation in proportion to her population. When world conditions are uncertain and trade interrupted, her people are plunged into depression.

Her big problem for the immediate future will be to regain markets interrupted by the war, and to find new customers as well. During the past year, business and agricultural interests have been planning for the future of foreign trade. The former have been actively promoting possible markets with Latin America, until now an area in which they did little business. The latter, acting on the theory that it is more important to receive a fair average price year after year, have negotiated agreements to sell their future wheat on a contract basis at $1.55 a bushel, forty cents below the current world price.

With less than six people per square mile, Canada is certainly far from overcrowded, and the likelihood of extensive settlement in the North is remote at present, unless wholesale immigration from Europe is resumed. Even then, the penetration will probably be gradual. None of the region east of Great Bear Lake can support communities based on agriculture. Distances are so tremendous and communications so costly, that the natural resources would have to be exceptionally valuable in order to justify the enormous expense involved.

The only section of the Northwest Territories that seems to offer likelihood of development is the Mackenzie River Valley. There the soil is fertile. Common vegetables grow well and small dairy farms are possible. Norman Wells can provide oil for heat and power, while the mineral wealth of the Great Bear-Great Slave region to the east seems unusually promising.

Yellowknife and Port Radium have proved to be not only experiments in mining under apparently impossible conditions, but they have provided experience for living in extremely unfavorable surroundings. The results seem to indicate that if sufficiently attractive economic reasons exist, it is possible to live there in relative comfort and contentment.

The most pressing domestic problem facing the Canadian people is the need for revising that portion of their constitution which deals with the powers delegated to the federal and provincial governments. The British North America Act has become outmoded and inadequate. Court decisions since 1867 have tended to reduce Dominion powers and to expand those of the provinces. Consequently, the provincial governments find themselves with large powers but without adequate means of financing them, while on the other hand, the federal government has revenue but lacks the power. Everybody agrees that something must be done about the situation.

The matter has been hanging in the balance for about ten years. During the war, the Dominion government was able to use its emergency powers to provide much needed laws for unemployment insurance and collective bargaining. With the return of peace, however, the responsibilities and revenues of the Dominion and the provinces becomes deadlocked once more. The Prime Minister called a Dominion-Provincial Conference in August of 1945, and laid before the members a plan whereby the federal government would assume responsibility for the costlier types of social legislation, such as unemployment relief, old age pensions, and health insurance, and pay twelve dollars per person annually to the provinces, in return for sole income and succession (inheritance) tax powers. When the provinces refused the offer on the grounds that they could not balance their budgets on the basis of that amount, the federal government raised the figure to fifteen dollars per person. Four conferences have been held in the past year, all without success. The public is becoming weary of the continuous bickering and lack of action. The governments must reach an agreement or face the danger of repeating the financial chaos of the thirties, yet provincial politicians continue to bargain for better terms.

The division between English and French-speaking peoples continues to be a distressing matter, and still contains the germs of trouble. A minority of both groups—loud-voiced, it is true—clamor for extreme measures. French ultra-nationalists may advocate an independent French republic, English-speaking extremists may urge shipping the French back to France, but such views are by no means universal, nor in any sense practical. There are those, French as well as English, who work earnestly and ceaselessly for national unity. It is only natural that French loyalty to Britain should be of a different sort than that held by people of Anglo-Saxon origin. To expect otherwise is to be unreasonable. However, it should not be inferred that French Canadians are less loyal citizens of Canada. Perhaps more than their English-speaking brethren, they have long been desirous of seeing Canada not as an appendage of Britain but as a nation in her own right.

The recent war has done much to bring British Canadians to the same view. Canada's achievements, military, financial, scientific, and industrial, have developed and intensified national feeling. Her people are taking a justifiable pride in their war record, and in the fact that they have met and discharged their responsibilities in full. They are more conscious of themselves as Canadians, as North Americans. In that respect the British and French have grown closer together in their ideals and aims for Canada. The recent law providing for Canadian, as distinguished from British citizenship, and the consideration recently given to the choice of a national flag are tangible proof of the growing spirit of nationalism.

The French with a longer span of history behind them have found themselves outnumbered in a country taken over by later settlers. Their adherence to their own civil law, language, and tradition, has contributed much toward erecting the barrier that exists. However, national unity and good will can never be realized until the French cease to feel that they are the target for discrimination. When French Canadians can enjoy equal opportunity in the provinces outside Quebec, when wages, labor conditions, social security in general, come under federal control, Canada will have gone far toward overcoming present, deep-rooted tensions.

People outside of Canada are frequently astonished to learn that in a nation of two major racial groups, many people can speak and understand only one language. The number of French who speak English is over twelve times greater than the corresponding group of British Canadians who speak French. However, a large number of both races (amounting to nearly half the population of the country) speak only their own language. Such knowledge as they acquire of each other is secondhand and often unreliable. The wonder is, not that there are differences and disagreements, but that they are not more frequent and more violent. Eminent Canadians have urged that the teaching of English be made compulsory in Quebec, and likewise the teaching of French in the other provinces. Thirty per cent of a population is a sizeable minority, and one that cannot be disregarded or dismissed with a shrug. The solution to Canada's race problem does not lie in molding all into a single pattern, but rather in fostering mutual respect and appreciation for each other's heritage and culture.

THE END

Index

◇◇

Acadia, founded, 58, 59; ceded to England, 67
Acadians, expulsion of, 19
Agriculture, 8-10, 11, 39-40, 113-115
Alberta, 35-37, 39, 40-42, 48
American Revolution, 71-72, 82
Anglo-French rivalry, 66-68
Annexation Manifesto, 88-89
Arvida, 30

Balfour Declaration, 113
Borden, Sir Robert Laird, 109-110, 111, 112
Bourassa, Henri, 109, 110
British Columbia, 43-49; agriculture, 46; climate, 43-44; early settlers, 44-46; fishing, 47; gold rush, 44-45; lumbering, 47-48; mining, 45
British Commonwealth Air Training Plan, 118-119
British Commonwealth of Nations, 112-113
British North America Act, 94, 96, 122-123

Calgary Stampede, 41-42
Canadian National Railway, 115
Canadian Pacific Railway, 98, 115
Canadian Shield, 2, 25, 29, 34, 36
Cariboo Road, 45
Carleton, Sir Guy (Baron Dorchester), 71
Cartier, Jacques, 26, 28, 58
C. C. F., 117
Champlain, Samuel de, 18, 25, 58, 59
Château clique, 83
Confederation, 94; causes of, 89-92; events leading up to, 91-94
Constitutional Act of 1791, 82
Continental Divide, 43
Cordilleran System, 43-44
Coureur de bois, 65

Depression, post war, effect on Canada, 116-117; political parties, 116-117; railroads, 115-116; wheat, 113-115
Dominion-Provincial conferences, 123
Duplessis, Maurice, 117
Durham's Report, 86

Education, 12-14

English Canadians, 6, 7, 11-12
Eskimos, 51-53

Family Compact, 83, 85
Fox farming, 21
Franklin, Benjamin, 72
Fraser, Simon, 80
French Canadians, 6-11; church, 9; homes and home life, 8, 10
French Nationalists, 109-110
Frontenac, Comte de, 31, 61-62, 63-64

Gaspé Peninsula, 25-26
Geographical regions, 3
Government, as English colony, 69-71, 72-73, 82-87; as French colony, 59-60, 68; compared and contrasted with United States, 94-96; Dominion organized, 89-90; responsible, 88

Habitants, 8
Halifax, 22, 23; founded, 18, 20, 69
Hudson, Henry, 77
Hudson's Bay Company, 38, 44, 51-52, 53, 77-79, 80, 81, 90
Hyde Park Declaration, 119

Industry, 8, 10
Inland waterways, 24
International Joint Commission, 107
Isolationism, 118

Jesuits, 60-61

King, William Lyon MacKenzie, 113

Labine, Gilbert, 54-57
Labor unions, 10-11
La Salle, 31
Laval-Montmorency, François Xavier de, 61-62
Laurier, Sir Wilfrid, 103-104, 105, 106-107, 109, 110
Louisburg, 17
Loyalists, 20, 30, 72-74

Macdonald, Sir John A., 97, 98, 102-103
MacKay, Donald, 22
Mackenzie, Alexander, 79
MacKenzie, William Lyon, 85, 113
Manitoba, 35-39, 40